THE Newlyweds' COOKBOOK

THE
Newlyweds'
COOKBOOK

RYLAND
PETERS
& SMALL
LONDON NEW YORK

Designer *Sarah Fraser*

Commissioning Editor *Elsa Petersen-Schepelern*

Editor *Sharon Cochrane*

Picture Research *Emily Westlake*

Production Manager *Patricia Harrington*

Art Director *Anne-Marie Bulat*

Publishing Director *Alison Starling*

Index *Hilary Bird*

First published in the United Kingdom in 2006
by Ryland Peters & Small
20–21 Jockey's Fields
London WC1R 4BW
www.rylandpeters.com

10 9 8 7 6 5 4

ISBN-13: 978 1 84172 963 3
ISBN-10: 1 84172 963 9

A CIP catalogue record for this book
is available from the British Library.

Printed in China

Notes

All spoon measurements are level unless otherwise
specified.

All eggs are medium unless otherwise specified. Uncooked
or partly cooked eggs should not be served to the very
young, the very old, those with compromised immune
systems or to pregnant women.

Ovens should be preheated to the specified temperature. If
using a fan-assisted oven, cooking times should be reduced
according to the manufacturer's instructions.

To sterilize preserving jars, wash them in hot, soapy water
and rinse in boiling water. Place in a large saucepan and
cover with hot water. With the saucepan lid on, bring the
water to the boil and continue boiling for 15 minutes. Turn
off the heat and leave the jars in the hot water until just
before they are to be filled. Invert the jars onto a clean tea
towel to dry. Sterilize the lids for 5 minutes, by boiling, or
according to the manufacturer's instructions. Jars should be
filled and sealed while they are still hot.

Contents

introduction

Getting married is one of the most exciting moments of your life. After the joys of the day itself, there are the delights of setting up home together. One of the many pleasures of married life is cooking for your loved one or, better still, preparing a meal together. You will no doubt receive a range of wonderful wedding gifts for your new home, for the first time in your lives you might own a decent set of saucepans or fabulous kitchen knives, as well as a complete set of dinner plates and dessert bowls. A well-equipped kitchen is sure to inspire you to cook up some delicious meals for your partner, family and friends.

This is where *The Newlyweds' Cookbook* comes into its own. It is a delicious source of culinary inspiration for every day of your new married life together. First, Kitchen Basics talks you through all the essential equipment and storecupboard items you will need in order to put a meal together. Then the recipe chapters cover everything from Brunch to Family Gatherings and Drinks. From quick weekday dinners that can be thrown together at the end of a busy day, to Special Occasions when you want to push the boat out and make something really memorable, this book is packed with ideas.

Sharing a meal with your loved one is an important part of daily life – on busy days, cooking and eating dinner may be the only chance you get to spend some time together and catch up with each other's news. You don't need to prepare a banquet every day, the simplest meal from the Quick Meals chapter can be made special just by eating it together. Cooking for friends and family should be a pleasure, and it can be with these easy-to-follow recipes that take the stress out of entertaining and virtually guarantee success. From all-time classic dishes to modern flavours, there is a host of ideas that are sure to impress. If you are new to cooking, begin with the recipes in the Quick Meals and Easy Entertaining chapters as these recipes are the simplest to prepare. However, all of the recipes in this book are easy to follow, so don't be afraid to try something new.

The Newlyweds' Cookbook is comprehensive and inspiring. It will become an invaluable cooking partner during your new married life and many of the recipes are destined to become family favourites in the years ahead. It is a book that will make cooking for your loved one, family and friends a true pleasure, whatever the occasion.

KITCHEN BASICS

Before you even begin cooking, there is essential equipment you will need to make your kitchen function as it should. You will find this listed on page 11. It is also a good idea to ensure your storecupboard is stocked with basic cooking ingredients so you always have them to hand when necessary. A well-stocked storecupboard will mean you can put together a meal in minutes on those really hectic days when you have no time to go shopping.

utensils, pots and pans

Whether you are a new cook or experienced in the kitchen, this list of essential equipment is what you will need to put the most basic of meals on the table. You may already have a number of these items, or received some of them as wedding gifts, so take all the equipment you already have out of the cupboards and drawers and lay it on the table. Check the list, opposite, to see if you have everything you need, then put it back in its place. If there's any equipment left on the table that you haven't used in the last 12 months, give it away. As funds allow, try to assemble all the equipment in the startup kit. Perhaps your friends and family can be persuaded to give you the items on the wish list for Christmas and birthdays.

Startup kit

For a basic set of equipment, buy the best you can afford, then it will last.

In your cupboards

1 non-stick frying pan

1 non-stick wok with lid

1 heavy shallow pan with ovenproof handles for stove-top or oven cooking

3 saucepans – small, medium and very large – with lids

1 collapsible metal steamer, bamboo steamer or 2-tier steaming saucepan

1 wire cooling rack

1 hand-held blender

1 sieve (strainer)

1 colander with legs or stand

1 box grater

1 set of mixing bowls

1 measuring jug

1 lemon squeezer

1 salad spinner

On the shelf

1 set of measuring scales

salt and pepper mills

1 cafetière and/or 1 teapot

In a block or wrap

1 paring or utility knife

1 large chopping knife

1 bread knife

1 pair of kitchen scissors

1 sharpening steel

On the work surface

1 heavy wooden chopping board

1 white heavy plastic board for raw meat and fish

1 roll of kitchen paper

In a large utensil pot

2 wooden spoons

1 large metal spoon

1 large slotted metal spoon

1 ladle

1 potato masher

1 long handled turner (fish slice)

2 plastic spatulas

1 set of salad servers

1 pair of tongs

In the top drawer

1 potato peeler

1 can opener

1 corkscrew

2 metal skewers

1 rolling pin

In the bottom drawer

greaseproof paper

aluminium foil

non-pvc food wrap

1 roll of medium freezer bags

1 roll of large heavy-duty bin bags

1 roll of kitchen string

tea towels

apron

oven gloves

For the oven

1 non-stick roasting tin

1 non-stick baking sheet

12-hole non-stick muffin tin

2 cake tins (20 cm diameter)

Wish list

Put these desirable objects on your 'wish list' for Christmas and birthdays.

In your cupboards

1 food processor

1 electric mixer

1 blender

1 stove-top grill pan

6 ramekins (150 ml)

3 glass bowls – small, medium and large

1 cooking thermometer

1 olive oil drizzler

1 mortar and pestle

In a large utensil pot

1 metal whisk

1 palette knife

1 meshed spoon for deep-frying

In the top drawer

parchment paper

1 roll of large freezer bags

1 pastry brush

In the bottom drawer

more tea towels (12 total)

another apron

another set of oven gloves

For the oven

another non-stick roasting tin

another non-stick baking sheet

1 loose-bottomed flan ring (25 cm diameter)

1 non-stick springform cake tin (20 cm diameter)

1 cake tin (18 cm square)

storecupboard essentials

It is a good idea to keep your storecupboard well stocked with useful ingredients that can be thrown together at a moment's notice to produce a quick meal. These are the essentials that are listed on the right. Fresh food should be bought often and in small quantities so it is always the freshest it can be. The food listed is just an illustration of the sorts of things you might want on hand at any one time.

Essentials

Staples

2–3 packets pasta, various shapes

2–3 packets rice – long grain, basmati, Thai fragrant, risotto

egg or rice noodles

dried lentils

plain and self-raising flour

baking powder

coffee, tea and sugar

Cans and cartons

vegetable bouillon (stock)

chicken bouillon (stock)

cans of: chopped tomatoes, chickpeas, cannellini and borlotti beans, anchovies in oil

coconut cream or milk

Oils and vinegars

large bottles of olive oil and sunflower oil

small bottles of extra virgin olive oil for salads, peanut oil for frying, chilli oil for flavouring

balsamic vinegar

Worcestershire sauce

red and white wine vinegar

Spices

whole nutmeg

ground cumin

ground coriander

ground turmeric

ground cinnamon and cinnamon sticks

sweet paprika

crushed dried chillies

Seasonings and flavourings

coarse sea salt

black peppercorns

soy sauce (light and dark)

Tabasco

teriyaki sauce

smooth Dijon mustard

clear honey

vanilla essence

Fresh food

a bag of onions

a head of garlic

2–3 red chillies

fresh ginger

fresh herbs, such as parsley

carrots

potatoes

tomatoes

lemons, limes, oranges, apples and pears

In the refrigerator

eggs

milk

unsalted butter

a wedge of Parmesan cheese

feta cheese

Greek yoghurt

In the freezer

vanilla ice cream

frozen peas

ice cubes

Extra items

When you've got the basics, begin adding these extra ingredients for more adventurous cooking.

Staples

couscous or cracked wheat

strong white bread flour

easy-blend dried yeast

jumbo oats

sultanas or raisins

cocoa powder

caster sugar

muscovado sugar

Oils and vinegars

small bottles of sesame oil and walnut oil

Spices

saffron threads

Seasonings and flavourings

Thai fish sauce

horseradish sauce

wholegrain mustard

English mustard powder

sun-dried tomatoes and peppers

black olives

capers

red wine

brandy

Marsala or sherry

Fresh food

your choice of other herbs, such as chives, basil, thyme and rosemary

crockery, glassware and cutlery

Now that you are married, you may well be entertaining family and friends more frequently than you did previously. Even when just the two of you are eating together, it's important to make mealtimes special from time to time, especially at the end of a long week or when you are celebrating a special occasion. Using your best table- and glassware can make even the simplest food look and taste amazing. You may have received a number of the items listed on the opposite page as wedding gifts, or own them already, but here is a list of the necessary glassware and tableware you will need to entertain a group of eight for dinner.

China

8 dinner plates

8 side plates

8 soup bowls

8 dessert plates or dishes

8 cups and saucers

Cutlery

8 dinner forks

8 salad forks

8 dinner knives

8 butter knives

8 steak knives

8 soup spoons

8 dessert spoons and/or forks

8 teaspoons

Serving pieces

2 ladles – 1 large and 1 small

sugar spoon or tongs

salad servers

1 large, three-pronged fork

2–3 serving spoons

pie slice

Serving dishes

2 platters – 1 large and 1 small

serving bowls – 3 sizes

sauce or gravy boat

water jug

cream jug

sugar bowl

teapot and/or coffee pot

small dishes, variety of

Glassware

8 water glasses

8 red wine glasses

8 white wine glasses

8 juice glasses

8 highball glasses

8 champagne flutes

8 brandy glasses

8 martini glasses

8 margarita glasses

8 liqueur glasses

Tableware

tablecloth

8 napkins

heatproof mats

BRUNCH

Breakfast during the week is often no more than a quick cup of coffee. The weekend offers a chance to enjoy a late start to the day with something delicious to eat. Preparing brunch for friends, your partner or family need not mean a hectic start to the day for you. Get organized the night before and you can relax with your guests and really enjoy a long, leisurely brunch.

making the perfect cup of coffee

Coffee plants grow in sub-tropical climates around the world. Their fruit looks similar to cherries but over six to nine months will ripen to a very dark brown. Each 'cherry' contains two coffee beans that are removed and then roasted; this caramelizes the sugars and carbohydrates in the bean and produces that distinctive flavour and aroma. How the beans are roasted will affect the flavour of the coffee. Dark roasted beans have a rather sharp, acidic flavour that is good for espresso, whereas lightly roasted beans have less caffeine and acidity and are best used in cafetières or filters.

Blending and grinding

Blending is a complex art, but also a matter of taste. A specialist coffee merchant will make a blend to suit your personal taste – experiment with different brands and blends and beans from various parts of the world until you find your perfect cup.

The beans are ground according to the method you use to make your coffee: use coarsely ground coffee for a percolator, medium ground for a drip filter or cafetière and fine ground for espresso machines. For really good, fresh coffee, grind your own beans and keep the beans in an airtight container in the refrigerator. If you buy your coffee ready-ground, buy only what you need for the week and store it in the refrigerator.

Making coffee

As a rough guide, use 2 tablespoons of freshly ground coffee per cup if using a cafetière, drip filter or espresso machine. Rinse the cafetière out with hot water, add the coffee and fill with freshly boiled water. Leave to steep for 3 minutes, then gently plunge. Follow the manufacturer's directions for espresso machines. If you prefer white coffee, serve it with scalded milk for a real treat.

making the perfect cup of tea

Teas are classified according to the quality of the leaves; the younger the leaves, the better the tea. Broken larger leaves are used in lesser teas. Leaves are treated in different ways to make various teas:

Green tea is unfermented but roasted immediately after harvesting to give a clear infusion with a delicate taste.

Black tea is fermented and dried, giving an infusion with a strong taste and rich amber colour. Varieties include Assam, Darjeeling and Lapsang Souchong.

Oolong tea is a semi-fermented leaf that is fragrant with a sweet aftertaste.

Scented tea comes in many varieties, the most famous of which is Earl Grey, a black tea with oil of bergamot added. Other scented teas may have flowers, fruit, leaves, stems or roots added.

Herbal teas or tisanes don't use real tea leaves. The many varieties include camomile and peppermint.

Making black, oolong or scented tea

Always use freshly boiled filtered water. Rinse out the teapot with the boiled water, then add the tea, allowing 1 teaspoon per person and 1 for the pot. Pour in the boiled water and leave to infuse for 3–5 minutes. Do not over-infuse the tea or it will become bitter and dark. How strong and what to add, if anything, is a matter of personal taste. Tea can be drunk black, or with a dash of cold milk, with sugar or a slice of lemon. Some people will only drink tea out of china mugs or cups – this is for you to choose.

Making green and herbal tea

These can be made in a mug for one person but if you are making tea for more than one, use a teapot. Green tea is best weak so calculate ½ teaspoon of tea per person, and the same for herbal. Many herbal teas come in individual bags and one of these per person is the best ratio. Brew for 1 minute – no longer or it will become bitter – then drink without milk or sugar.

This is so yummy – a gooey, sweet, fruity porridge made with a homemade granola or muesli mix, soaked overnight in cinnamon-infused milk. Add whatever berries or soft fruits take your fancy.

cinnamon-soaked granola
with fresh fruits

400 ml full-fat milk, plus extra to serve

½ teaspoon ground cinnamon

2 tablespoons clear honey

200 g fresh fruit and berries, such as strawberries, raspberries and peaches

granola

200 g rolled oats

50 g oatmeal

50 g oat bran

150 g mixed nuts, such as hazelnuts, almonds, macadamias and cashews, toasted and chopped

2 tablespoons sunflower seeds

2 tablespoons pumpkin seeds

2 tablespoons sesame seeds

50 g raisins

100 g mixed dried fruits, chopped, such as apricots, figs, dates, banana and mango

serves 4

To make the granola, put the oats in a dry frying pan and toast over medium heat, stirring, until golden. Transfer to a large bowl. Repeat with the oatmeal, oat bran, nuts and seeds, in separate batches. Let cool, then add the raisins and dried fruits and store in an airtight container. Alternatively, don't toast the ingredients; just put all the granola ingredients in a large bowl, mix well and transfer to an airtight container. You will need 300 g granola or untoasted muesli for this recipe, the remainder can be stored in the airtight container for up to 2 weeks.

Put the milk, cinnamon and honey in a saucepan. Heat until almost boiling, then remove from the heat.

Divide 300 g granola between 4 cereal bowls. Pour over the hot milk, let cool, then refrigerate overnight. Serve at room temperature, topped with fresh fruit and berries of your choice and extra milk.

Try to buy figs as ripe as possible for this recipe. If they are unavailable, use other fruits such as peaches or apricots.

fresh figs *with ricotta & honeycomb*

Arrange the figs and ricotta on a large plate and serve the honeycomb or honey in a separate bowl for everyone to help themselves.

500 g fresh ripe figs, about 8

500 g ricotta cheese, sliced

a piece of honeycomb or 4–8 tablespoons clear honey

serves 4

Here is a classic brunch dish with a twist! If you don't have a waffle iron, simply drop a ladle of batter onto a lightly greased, heated frying pan and fry on both sides until golden.

waffles *with maple syrup ice cream*

ice cream

500 ml double cream

250 ml milk

seeds from 1 vanilla pod

5 egg yolks (to separate eggs, see page 147)

125 ml maple syrup, plus extra to serve

waffles

150 g plain flour

1 teaspoon baking powder

½ teaspoon bicarbonate of soda

1 tablespoon caster sugar

125 ml buttermilk

1 egg, lightly beaten

75 g butter, melted

an ice cream maker (optional)

a waffle iron, lightly greased

serves 6

To make the ice cream, put the cream, milk and vanilla seeds in a saucepan and heat until the mixture reaches boiling point. Remove from the heat and set aside.

Meanwhile, put the egg yolks and maple syrup in a bowl and beat to mix. Stir in the heated cream mixture and return to the pan. Heat gently, stirring, until it thickens enough to coat the back of a wooden spoon. Do not let the mixture boil or it will curdle. Remove the pan from the heat and let cool.

Freeze in an ice cream maker, following the manufacturer's instructions. If you don't have an ice cream maker, pour the mixture into flat freezer trays and put them in the freezer. Let the mixture partially freeze, then remove from the freezer, beat to break up the ice crystals and return the trays to the freezer. Repeat several times – the more you do it, the smoother the end result.

To make the waffles, sift the flour, baking powder and bicarbonate of soda into a bowl. Stir in the sugar. In a second bowl, beat the the buttermilk, egg and butter together, then add to the dry ingredients and beat until smooth. Spoon a layer of the batter into a heated waffle iron and spread flat. Cook for about 1 minute until crisp and golden. Serve hot with a scoop of ice cream and a little extra maple syrup poured over. Repeat with the remaining waffle batter.

american pancakes

250 g plain flour

2 teaspoons baking powder

1 teaspoon sea salt

3 tablespoons sugar

250 ml milk

2 eggs, lightly beaten

50 g unsalted butter, melted, plus extra for cooking

maple butter syrup

80 ml maple syrup

25 g unsalted butter

a cast-iron frying pan or flat-surfaced griddle

makes 8–12, serves 4

Sift the flour, baking powder, salt and sugar into a bowl. Mix the milk, eggs and the melted butter in a large jug, then add the flour mixture and mix quickly to make a batter (don't worry about lumps – they're good). Alternatively, make the batter in a bowl and transfer to a jug.

Heat a cast-iron frying pan or flat-surfaced griddle until medium hot, grease lightly with extra butter and pour in the batter in batches to make rounds, 8–10 cm diameter. Cook for 1–2 minutes or until bubbles form on top of the pancakes and the undersides are is golden, then flip each one over and cook for 1 minute more. Keep the pancakes warm in a low oven while you cook the remaining batches.

To make the maple butter syrup, heat the maple syrup and butter together in a small saucepan or microwave until the butter has melted. Stack the pancakes on warmed plates and pour over the buttery syrup. Serve immediately.

orange & bitter chocolate muffins

Nothing beats a home-baked muffin with a cup of steaming coffee or tea for a special treat.

280 g plain flour
1½ teaspoons baking powder
1 teaspoon salt
½ teaspoon bicarbonate of soda
225 g caster sugar
100 g plain chocolate (at least 70 per cent cocoa solids), coarsely chopped
grated zest and juice of 1 unwaxed orange
55 g butter
175 ml milk

a 12-hole muffin tin, preferably non-stick, lightly greased

makes 12 muffins

Sift the flour, baking powder, salt and bicarbonate of soda into a large bowl. Stir in the sugar, chopped chocolate and orange zest and make a well in the centre of the dry ingredients.

Put the butter in a small saucepan and heat until melted. Remove the pan from the heat, then stir in the milk and orange juice. Pour the butter and orange mixture into the well of the dry ingredients and stir briefly with a wooden spoon. Do not overmix – the batter should be lumpy, not smooth. Spoon the batter into the prepared tin, filling each hole three-quarters full.

Bake in a preheated oven at 190°C (375°F) Gas 5 for about 20 minutes until golden and cooked through. (Insert a skewer into the middle of one muffin to test – the skewer should come out clean.)

Remove the muffins from the oven and let cool in the tin for a couple of minutes, then turn them out onto a wire rack to cool slightly. Serve warm or at room temperature.

blueberry muffins

Though they're best eaten hot from the oven, muffins can be made the night before, left to cool, stored in an airtight container, then reheated before serving.

250 g plain flour
1 teaspoon baking powder
¼ teaspoon fine sea salt
200 g caster sugar
2 eggs, lightly beaten
65 g butter, melted, or 80 ml sunflower oil
1 teaspoon pure vanilla essence
125 ml low-fat plain yoghurt
200 g blueberries

a 6-hole or 12-hole muffin tin, preferably non-stick, lightly greased

makes 6 large or 12 small muffins

Sift the flour and baking powder into a bowl and stir in the salt. Add all the remaining ingredients and fold together until just blended; do not beat or overmix. Spoon the batter into the prepared tin, filling each hole three-quarters full.

Bake in a preheated oven at 180°C (350°F) Gas 4 for 20–30 minutes, until golden and firm to the touch. (Insert a skewer into the middle of one muffin to test – the skewer should come out clean.) Remove the muffins from the oven and let cool in the tin for a couple of minutes, then turn them out onto a wire rack to cool slightly. Serve warm or at room temperature.

Greasing, flouring and lining baking tins

- *'Greasing' means brushing the inside of the tin with a thin film of butter or oil. This stops the food from sticking to the tin when cooked.*

- *Also to stop the food sticking, tins are sometimes then dusted with a light layer of flour, or lined with baking parchment on the base, or on the base and sides.*

- *Lining is usually done if the food is to be baked for a long time, such as a large fruit cake.*

Charring the asparagus spears on a stove-top grill pan
intensifies their flavour and adds a smokiness to the frittata.

charred asparagus & herb frittata
with smoked salmon

250 g asparagus spears, trimmed

1 tablespoon extra virgin olive oil

6 free-range eggs

4 spring onions, finely chopped

2 tablespoons chopped fresh
herbs, such as tarragon and mint

50 g ricotta cheese

15 g butter

sea salt and cracked black pepper

to serve

250 g smoked salmon, thinly sliced

crème fraîche

lemon wedges

a stove-top grill pan

serves 4

Toss the asparagus with the oil and a little salt and pepper. Heat a stove-top grill pan until hot, add the asparagus and cook for 3–4 minutes, turning until evenly charred. Let cool.

Put the eggs in a bowl and beat until evenly mixed. Stir in the spring onions, herbs, ricotta and salt and pepper to taste.

Melt the butter in a large non-stick frying pan, add the egg mixture and swirl to the edge of the pan. Arrange the asparagus spears over the top and cook for 3–4 minutes until the eggs are set underneath.

Put the pan briefly under a hot grill to cook the top of the frittata, then remove from the heat and let cool to room temperature.

Cut the frittata into wedges and serve with the smoked salmon, crème fraîche and lemon pieces.

Creamy scrambled eggs topped with rocket pesto
are especially good on top of a crunchy nut bread.

creamy eggs *with rocket pesto*

To make the rocket pesto, chop the rocket leaves coarsely, then transfer to a food processor. Add the basil, almonds, oil, garlic, salt and pepper and purée briefly to form a vivid green paste. Transfer to a bowl and stir in the cheese. Set aside.

Put the eggs and cream in a bowl, whisk with a fork, then add salt and pepper, to taste. Put the butter in a large non-stick saucepan, melt gently, then add the egg mixture and cook over low heat, stirring with a wooden spoon until the eggs have just set.

Put a slice of toast onto each plate, top with the scrambled eggs and serve immediately, with a spoonful of rocket pesto.

12 free-range eggs

4 tablespoons double cream

50 g butter

6 slices bread, toasted (preferably walnut bread)

sea salt and freshly ground black pepper

rocket pesto

50 g rocket

2 tablespoons chopped fresh basil leaves

2 tablespoons blanched almonds, chopped

100 ml extra virgin olive oil

1 garlic clove, chopped

2 tablespoons freshly grated pecorino or Parmesan cheese

serves 6

Smoked salmon and baked eggs make the perfect breakfast treat
– it's an easy, elegant dish that takes no time at all.

baked eggs
with smoked salmon & chives

200 g smoked salmon slices, chopped

1 tablespoon chopped fresh chives

4 free-range eggs

4 tablespoons double cream

freshly ground black pepper

toast, to serve

4 ramekins or shallow dishes, 200 ml each, well buttered

serves 4

Divide the smoked salmon and chives among the 4 buttered ramekins. Make a small indent in the salmon with the back of a spoon and break an egg into the hollow. Sprinkle with a little pepper and spoon the cream over the top.

Put the ramekins in a roasting tin and half-fill the tin with boiling water. Bake in a preheated oven at 180°C (350°F) Gas 4 for 10–15 minutes until the eggs have just set. Remove from the oven, let cool for a few minutes, then serve with toast.

Try substituting smoked salmon for the ham or, for vegetarians, replace the ham with wilted spinach.

eggs benedict

4 large slices of Parma ham

1 tablespoon vinegar

4 free-range eggs

4 plain English muffins

sea salt and cracked black pepper

hollandaise sauce

3 free-range egg yolks (to separate eggs, see page 147)

2 tablespoons water

1 teaspoon freshly squeezed lemon juice

250 g unsalted butter, melted

serves 4

To make the hollandaise sauce, put the egg yolks, water and lemon juice in a blender and process until frothy. With the motor running, gradually pour in the melted butter in a steady stream until the sauce is thickened and glossy. Transfer the sauce to a heatproof bowl set over a saucepan of hot water. Cover and keep the sauce warm.

Grill or fry the slices of ham until really crisp and keep them warm in a low oven. To poach the eggs, bring a saucepan of lightly salted water to the boil. Add the vinegar and reduce the heat so the water simmers gently. Swirl the water well with a fork and crack 2 eggs into the water. Cook for 3 minutes, then remove with a slotted spoon. Repeat with the remaining 2 eggs.

Meanwhile, toast the muffins whole. Top each one with a slice of crispy ham, then a poached egg. Spoon over the hollandaise sauce, sprinkle with salt and pepper and serve at once.

This is a good substantial brunch dish and makes great comfort food. Roasting the tomatoes really brings out their juicy flavours and they make the perfect partner for the crispy potatoes.

hash browns *with sausages & oven roasted tomatoes*

Cook the potatoes in a large saucepan of lightly salted, boiling water for 10–12 minutes, until almost cooked through. Drain well and mash roughly.

Melt the butter in a large non-stick frying pan, add the onion and fry gently for 15 minutes until soft and golden. Add the potatoes to the pan with salt and pepper, to taste. Cook, stirring and mashing the potatoes occasionally, for 15–20 minutes until well browned and crispy around the edges.

Meanwhile, put the sausages in a roasting tin, drizzle with half the oil and roast on the middle shelf of a preheated oven at 200°C (400°F) Gas 6 for 25 minutes.

Put the tomatoes, still on the vine, in an ovenproof dish. Drizzle with the remaining oil and put on the top shelf of the oven after the sausages have been cooking for 5 minutes. Cook the tomatoes for 15 minutes, then drizzle over the balsamic vinegar and cook for 5 minutes more.

Spoon the hash browns onto warmed plates and top with the sausages, tomatoes and their juice. Serve immediately.

750 g floury potatoes, such as Desirée, peeled and diced

50 g butter

1 large onion, finely chopped

12 good-quality sausages

2 tablespoons olive oil

500 g cherry tomatoes, on the vine

1 tablespoon balsamic vinegar

sea salt and freshly ground black pepper

serves 4

mushrooms on toast
with melted cheese

Large, juicy portobellos need little embellishment – just a slice of cheese and a hint of sweetness from the brioche.

Melt the butter in a saucepan, add the mushrooms and cook for about 10 minutes, until golden and beginning to release their juices. Add salt and pepper, to taste.

Meanwhile, toast the brioche or bread slices on both sides under a preheated grill. Spoon over the mushrooms and their juices and top with the Taleggio slices. Return the topped brioche to the grill for a few seconds, so that the cheese just begins to melt. Serve at once.

125 g butter

8 large portobello mushrooms, wiped and trimmed

4 slices of brioche or multigrain bread

125 g Taleggio cheese, sliced

sea salt and freshly ground black pepper

serves 4

kick-starter bloody mary

crushed ice
5 lemons
200 ml vodka
7 cm white horseradish, freshly grated,
or 1 tablespoon bottled horseradish
1 tablespoon Worcestershire sauce
1 teaspoon Tabasco sauce
750 ml tomato juice, well chilled
freshly ground black pepper
celery sticks, with leaves, to serve

serves 4

If you or your guests can't face alcohol so early in the day, make one jug of this drink and one jug of Virgin Mary (see page 175), which is made without the vodka.

Half-fill a large jug with crushed ice. Cut 1 lemon into slices and squeeze the juice from the others. Add the lemons and the juice to the jug, together with all the other ingredients except the celery. Mix well. Serve in 4 highball glasses with a celery stick.

tropical smoothie

1 ripe mango
1 ripe banana,
coarsely chopped
grated zest and juice of
1 unwaxed lime
4 tablespoons freshly
squeezed orange juice

serves 2

Use a juicy, ripe mango to make this smoothie – it should be really fragrant.

To slice the mango, cut off both ends of the fruit either side of the stone. Peel back the skin and, at the same time, scoop out the flesh with a spoon. Cut the flesh into slices. Peel off the remaining skin from the mango and, using a knife, cut as much flesh as you can from the stone. Put the mango slices, banana, lime zest and juice and orange juice in a blender or food processor and process until smooth. Pour into 2 tall glasses and serve at once.

very berry smoothie

125 g strawberries, hulled
125 g raspberries
50 g blueberries
200 ml cranberry juice
4 tablespoons Greek yoghurt
1 teaspoon clear honey
4 large ice cubes

serves 2

The yoghurt in this bright, summery smoothie adds a creamy taste and colour to the red berries. Add more or less honey, depending on how sweet your tooth is.

Put 2 tall glasses in the freezer to chill.

Put all the ingredients in a blender or food processor and process until almost smooth. Taste for sweetness, adding more honey, if needed. Pour into the 2 chilled glasses and serve immediately.

SNACKS, STARTERS & SALADS

These little dishes can be served at any time of the day. They are perfect for lunch, whether you are looking for a quick snack or a more leisurely meal to be enjoyed with family and friends. Many can be used as a starter, or as a snack when you get home late and need something satisfying to eat, as well as something quick and easy to prepare.

pan-grilled bruschetta
with onion marmalade & goats' cheese

2 ciabatta rolls, halved crossways

4 large handfuls of mixed salad leaves

I tablespoon extra virgin olive oil, plus extra for serving

4 tablespoons Red Onion Marmalade (see page 181)

125 g soft, mild goats' cheese

sea salt and freshly ground black pepper

a stove-top grill pan

serves 4

Char-grilled bread is more than just toast – it stays chewy on the inside, has a smoky flavour and lovely stripes from the grill pan.

Heat a stove-top grill pan until hot. Add the ciabatta and cook for 1–2 minutes on each side until lightly toasted and charred.

Meanwhile, put the salad leaves in a bowl, add the olive oil and salt and pepper to taste. Toss well.

Transfer the toasted ciabatta to serving plates. Spread with the red onion marmalade, then add a handful of salad leaves and crumble the goats' cheese on top. Sprinkle with olive oil and lots of black pepper and serve.

This is such a classic sandwich and a really delicious one at that! Always use the freshest bread for this snack and choose a nice crusty loaf, if you can.

steak & tomato sandwich

olive oil, for greasing

4 sirloin steaks, 100 g each

8 slices of bread

butter, for spreading

4 teaspoons Dijon mustard

2 beef tomatoes, sliced

2 bunches of rocket, about 100 g

sea salt and freshly ground black pepper

a stove-top grill pan (optional)

serves 4

Brush a stove-top grill pan or a non-stick frying pan with a little olive oil and heat until hot. Add the steaks to the pan and cook for 1 minute on each side for rare steak, 2 minutes each side for medium or 3 minutes each side for well done.

Spread 4 slices of the bread with butter and mustard, then add the sliced tomatoes and rocket.

Top with the cooked steak and sprinkle with salt and pepper. Butter the remaining slices of bread and put them on top of the steaks. Press together and serve.

250 g boneless pork shoulder, minced

250 g pork belly, minced

500 g veal, minced

200 g calves' liver, finely chopped

I egg, beaten

2 shallots, finely chopped

2 garlic cloves, crushed

I tablespoon coarse sea salt

2 tablespoons green peppercorns in brine, drained, plus extra for decorating

½ teaspoon ground allspice

3 tablespoons Cognac

a handful of fresh bay leaves (see method)

freshly ground black pepper

to serve

French cornichons

sliced baguette

unsalted butter

a rectangular terrine mould, 30 x 11 cm

serves 10–12

This terrine is simplicity itself. If you ask your butcher to mince all the meat, except the liver, then it will be even easier. Serve in slices to begin an informal meal, with plenty of fresh baguette, unsalted butter and French cornichons.

rustic pâté *with green peppercorns*

Put the pork shoulder and belly, veal and liver in a large bowl. Add the egg, shallots, garlic, salt, black pepper, green peppercorns, allspice and Cognac and mix well, preferably with your hands.

Fill the mould with the meat mixture, patting to spread evenly. Arrange bay leaves on top of the mould and dot with extra green peppercorns. Set the mould in a roasting tin and add enough boiling water to come halfway up the sides of the mould. Cover the terrine with foil and bake in a preheated oven at 180°C (350°F) Gas 4 until a knife inserted in the middle is hot to the touch after 30 seconds, about 1½ hours.

Remove from the oven and let cool. When the pâté is at room temperature, cover with baking parchment and put a few food cans on top to weigh the pâté down. Refrigerate, with the weights on top, for at least 1 day, but ideally for 3. The pâté will keep, refrigerated, for 1 week. Bring to room temperature before serving with French cornichons, slices of baguette and butter.

warm chunky fish pâté

This shouldn't be a smooth pâté, so flake the cooked fish into big pieces.

Put the salmon, skin side up, in a shallow microwavable dish. Add the wine and cover with microwave-safe clingfilm. Cook on MEDIUM for 5 minutes.

Meanwhile, put the cream cheese, yoghurt, dill and lemon juice in a large bowl and mix well.

Drain the fish on kitchen paper and flake into large pieces. Gently fold the fish into the cream cheese mixture and season to taste with salt and pepper. Serve the pâté with toast and lemon wedges.

150 g salmon fillet, skin on

150 ml white wine

125 g cream cheese

4 tablespoons Greek yoghurt

2 tablespoons coarsely chopped fresh dill

a squeeze of fresh lemon juice

sea salt and freshly ground black pepper

to serve

black rye bread, toasted

I lemon, cut into wedges

serves 4

aubergine antipasto *with pine nuts & herbs*

2–3 medium aubergines,
about 750 g

2 tablespoons sea salt

125 ml extra virgin olive oil

50 g pine nuts

1 small bunch of mint,
half chopped, half in sprigs

1 small bunch of flat leaf parsley,
half chopped, half in sprigs

2 tablespoons aged
balsamic vinegar

freshly ground black pepper

a stove-top grill pan

serves 4-6

A simple, delicious snack or starter, with mellow olive oil accentuating the flavours.

Slice the aubergines lengthways into 1 cm slices. Score both sides of each slice with a fork. Sprinkle with salt. Let drain on a rack for 20 minutes, then pat dry with kitchen paper.

Heat a stove-top grill pan until very hot. Wipe the pan with olive oil using a wad of crumpled kitchen paper or a heatproof brush. Brush each slice of aubergine with olive oil. Press the aubergine down firmly on the hot pan and cook for 3–5 minutes on each side, in batches if necessary, until grill-marked, tender and aromatic. Heat 1 tablespoon olive oil in a frying pan, add the pine nuts and toast gently until golden. Remove from the pan and set aside.

Scatter the cooked aubergine with chopped mint, chopped parsley, pepper and a few drops of balsamic vinegar. Loop the slices on serving plates, add the pine nuts and sprigs of mint and parsley and serve.

spanish potato omelette

Heat the oil in a medium frying pan, add the potatoes and onion and cook over low heat for 12–14 minutes or until tender but not browned, moving them about with a fish slice so they cook evenly. Add the garlic, if using, for the last 2 minutes.

Put the eggs, salt and pepper in a bowl and beat well. Using a slotted spoon, remove the cooked potatoes and garlic from the pan and stir it into the egg mixture. Stir in the chopped parsley or spring onion tops. Quickly pour the egg mixture back into the hot frying pan. Cook, not stirring, over low to moderate heat for 4–5 minutes or until firm, but do not let it brown too much. The top will still be wobbly, only part-cooked.

Holding a heatproof plate over the top of the omelette, quickly invert the pan, omelette and plate. Slide the hot omelette, upside down, back into the pan to brown the other side for 2–3 minutes more. Remove from the pan and let cool for 5 minutes.

To make the sauce, put the piquillos, 6 tablespoons of the liquid from the can (make it up with water if necessary) and the sherry vinegar in a blender. Purée to form a smooth, scarlet sauce. Cut the omelette into wedges or cubes. Serve the sauce separately, spooning some over the omelette.

100 ml extra virgin olive oil

1 kg salad potatoes, peeled
and cut into 2 cm cubes

1 onion, sliced into rings

4 garlic cloves, finely
chopped (optional)

6 eggs

4 tablespoons chopped fresh
flat leaf parsley or spring
onion tops

sea salt and freshly ground
black pepper

piquillo sauce

225 g can or jar of roasted
piquillo peppers or pimientos

3 tablespoons sherry vinegar

serves 4-6

This classic French soup is ideal when it's chilly outside and people are hungry inside.

french onion soup

50 g unsalted butter

I tablespoon extra virgin olive oil

3 large onions, about 1.3 kg, thinly sliced

2 garlic cloves, crushed

I tablespoon plain flour

I litre beef or chicken stock

600 ml dry white wine

I fresh bay leaf

2 sprigs of fresh thyme

I baguette, or other white bread, sliced

about 180 g freshly grated Gruyère cheese

coarse sea salt and freshly ground black pepper

a baking sheet

serves 4-6

Put the butter and oil in a large saucepan and melt over medium heat. Add the onions and cook over low heat until soft, 15–20 minutes.

Add the garlic and flour and cook, stirring, for about 1 minute. Add the stock, wine, bay leaf and thyme. Season with salt and pepper and bring to the boil. Boil for 1 minute, then lower the heat and simmer very gently for 20 minutes. Taste and adjust the seasoning with salt and pepper, if necessary. At this point, the soup will be cooked, but standing time will improve the flavour – at least 30 minutes.

Before serving, preheat the grill. Put the baguette slices on a baking sheet and brown under the grill until lightly toasted. Set aside.

To serve, reheat the soup, then ladle it into ovenproof bowls. Top with a few toasted baguette slices, sprinkle grated cheese over the top and cook under the hot grill until the cheese is browned and bubbling. Serve immediately.

butternut squash soup

The key to this soup is the light spicing and the roasting of the butternut squash to bring out its sweet flavour.

Put the butternut squash halves flesh side down on the baking sheet. Roast in a preheated oven at 190°C (375°F) Gas 5 for 45 minutes or until tender. Remove from the oven and, using a spoon, scoop the flesh out of the skins into a bowl. Discard the skins.

Put the butter in a large saucepan and melt over medium to low heat. Add the leek, bay leaf, peppercorns and allspice and fry gently until the leek begins to soften. Add the butternut squash, stock and 1 litre water. Bring to the boil, reduce the heat and simmer for about 10 minutes, or until the leeks are very soft.

Remove the bay leaf and transfer the soup to a blender. Add the toasted pine nuts and blend until smooth, working in batches if necessary. Return the soup to the saucepan and reheat. Serve hot with crusty bread.

I butternut squash, halved lengthways and deseeded

25 g unsalted butter

I large leek, trimmed and chopped

I fresh bay leaf

a few black peppercorns, crushed

4–5 allspice berries, crushed

600 ml Vegetable Stock (see page 178)

60 g pine nuts, toasted in a dry frying pan

crusty bread, to serve

a non-stick baking sheet

serves 4

750 g ripe vine tomatoes

I large shallot, or I small red onion, thinly sliced

coarse sea salt and freshly ground black pepper

anchovy vinaigrette

I garlic clove

½ teaspoon Dijon mustard

2 tablespoons white wine vinegar

6 anchovy fillets, packed in oil

8 tablespoons extra virgin olive oil

a small handful of fresh basil leaves

to serve

a handful of fresh flat leaf parsley, finely chopped

a few fresh basil leaves, torn

serves 4

'Anchoïade' is a Provençal anchovy sauce/dip that is spread thickly on grilled bread slices or served with raw vegetables as a starter. Here it is used as a dressing for what will hopefully be very ripe, flavourful tomatoes. If these are not available, use boiled new potatoes instead.

tomato salad *with anchovy vinaigrette*

To make the vinaigrette, put the garlic, mustard, vinegar and anchovies in a small food processor and blend well. Add the oil, I tablespoon at a time, then blend in the basil. Season with pepper and set aside.

Cut the tomatoes into quarters or eighths, depending on their size. Arrange them on a plate and sprinkle with the shallot. Season lightly with salt, then spoon the vinaigrette over the top. Sprinkle with the parsley, basil and some black pepper, and serve at room temperature.

2 red peppers, halved and deseeded

2 yellow peppers, halved and deseeded

500 g ripe plum tomatoes

4 tablespoons red wine vinegar

2 garlic cloves, crushed to a paste with coarse sea salt

125 ml extra virgin olive oil, plus extra for drizzling

2 tablespoons capers

75 g black olives, pitted

I small or ½ large loaf day-old ciabatta, cut coarsely into cubes

a bunch of basil, leaves torn

freshly ground black pepper

a baking sheet

serves 4–6

tuscan panzanella

The bread will drink up the rich flavours of the dressing, so use a crusty, firm-crumbed bread, such as ciabatta.

Put the peppers cut side down on a baking sheet and grill under a preheated hot grill until blistered and charred. Transfer to a plastic bag, seal and let cool (the steam will loosen the skin, making it easier to peel). Scrape off the skin, then cut the peppers into strips, reserving any juice.

Halve the tomatoes and scoop out the cores and seeds over a bowl to catch the juice. Purée the cores and seeds in a blender, then press the extra juice through a sieve into the bowl. Discard the pulp and seeds. Cut the tomato halves into strips.

Put the tomato juice, vinegar, garlic and black pepper in a bowl. Gradually add the olive oil, whisking until blended.

Put the pepper and tomato strips in a bowl, add the capers, olives, ciabatta and basil and mix. Add the tomato dressing, toss well to coat, then set aside for I hour to develop the flavours. Drizzle with extra olive oil and serve.

This shouldn't be made too far in advance, or the salad will go soggy and the avocado will discolour.

bacon, avocado & feta salad

16 slices of bacon

300 g mixed salad leaves

3 ripe avocados, sliced

4 ripe tomatoes, cut into wedges

200 g feta cheese, about 50 g per person

a large handful of fresh flat leaf parsley, roughly chopped

a large handful of fresh coriander, roughly chopped

freshly ground black pepper

dressing

4 tablespoons wine vinegar

½ teaspoon fine sea salt

1½ teaspoons Dijon mustard

175–200 ml extra virgin olive oil

serves 4

Cook the bacon in a hot non-stick frying pan until crisp. Drain on kitchen paper and set aside.

To make the dressing, put the vinegar and salt in a small bowl. Using a small whisk or fork, stir until the salt dissolves. Whisk in the mustard, then gradually whisk in the oil, 1 tablespoon at a time. Taste when you've added 12 tablespoons. If it's too sharp, add a few more tablespoons, whisking well.

Put the salad leaves in a large bowl and add about 6 tablespoons of the dressing – the leaves should be just coated, not drowning. Toss well, then divide the leaves among 4 plates.

Cut each slice of bacon into 3–4 pieces and share between the plates, on top of the leaves (about 4 slices per plate). Arrange equal amounts of avocado and tomato on each plate. Divide the feta into 4 portions and crumble it over each serving. Sprinkle with the parsley and coriander. Trickle the remaining dressing over the top and finish with a generous grinding of black pepper. Serve.

peppered goats' cheese

Cheese – especially blue, goats' milk or creamy – makes excellent salads. Gentle cooking gives this one extra pizzazz.

Sprinkle the pepper onto a plate. Lightly press both sides of each cheese half into the pepper to coat.

Heat a stove-top grill pan until hot. Add the peppered cheese slices, cut side down, and cook for 2 minutes. Turn them over, cover loosely with foil and cook for a further 4–5 minutes until the cheese is soft but not melted.

Put the rocket, spinach, oil and lemon juice in a large bowl. Add salt to taste and toss to coat. Divide the salad among 4 large serving plates or flat bowls and top with a slice of grilled cheese. Sprinkle with chilli oil, if using, and serve.

1 tablespoon freshly ground black pepper

2 goats' cheeses, 100 g each, with rind, halved crossways

2 large handfuls of wild rocket

2 large handfuls of baby leaf spinach

1 tablespoon extra virgin olive oil

freshly squeezed juice of ½ lemon

sea salt

Chilli Oil, to serve (optional, see page 181)

a stove-top grill pan

serves 4

italian mixed salad

If you ask for a mixed salad in Italy, this is what you will get. Oil and vinegar are served at the table so you can dress the salad yourself.

350 g waxy potatoes, peeled
175 g fine green beans, trimmed
about 1 tablespoon extra virgin olive oil
50 g black or green olives, pitted
1 small crisp lettuce
2 large ripe tomatoes, quartered (or unripe to be authentic)
3 tablespoons chopped fresh parsley
sea salt and freshly ground black pepper

to serve
a small bottle of good olive oil
a small bottle of red wine vinegar

serves 4

Boil the potatoes in a saucepan of lightly salted boiling water for about 15 minutes or until tender, adding the beans 4 minutes before the potatoes are ready. Drain and cover with cold water to stop the vegetables cooking.

When cold, drain well. Transfer the beans to a bowl, slice the potatoes thickly and add to the beans, moistening with a little olive oil. Add the olives and toss well.

Wash the lettuce and tear into bite-sized pieces. Add the lettuce and tomatoes to the potatoes and beans and toss lightly. Transfer to a serving bowl and sprinkle with parsley, salt and pepper. Serve the olive oil and vinegar separately and dress the salad at the table.

Washing and drying salad leaves

- *Wash crisp-leafed lettuces and other salad leaves in a bowl of water, transfer to a salad spinner and spin dry. Wrap in a cloth or kitchen paper and store in the refrigerator – the leaves will become even crisper.*
- *Rinse soft-leafed greens, such as lamb's lettuce or rocket just before using and let drain in a colander. Pat dry with kitchen paper and serve as soon as possible.*

---

salade niçoise

This classic French salad is extremely versatile – it is delicious served as a lunch, a starter or even as a one-dish supper.

400 g tuna steak, cut into 4 pieces
4 medium new potatoes, cooked and sliced
4 tomatoes, skinned* and cut into wedges
100 g French beans, trimmed, halved and cooked
1 red onion, sliced
4 baby lettuces, such as Little Gem, quartered lengthways
4 hard-boiled eggs, peeled and halved
4 anchovies, cut into long strips
12 black olives, pitted
a bunch of flat leaf parsley, roughly chopped
4 tablespoons olive oil
4 tablespoons balsamic vinegar
sea salt and freshly ground black pepper
1 lemon, cut into wedges, to serve

a stove-top grill pan (optional)

serves 4

Heat a stove-top grill pan or an overhead grill, add the tuna and cook for 1–2 minutes on each side. Remove from the heat, set aside and keep it warm.

Put the cooked sliced potatoes in a bowl with the tomato wedges, beans, onion, lettuce and eggs. Add the anchovies, olives, parsley, olive oil, balsamic vinegar and salt and pepper, to taste. Mix carefully.

Put the tuna on top of the salad and serve with wedges of lemon. Alternatively, the traditional way to serve this salad is to arrange groups of the ingredients on a large platter, drizzle with the olive oil and vinegar, then serve.

*Note To skin tomatoes, bring a saucepan of water to the boil, cut a cross in the skin at the base of each tomato, then plunge them into the boiling water for just 20 seconds. Drain, then peel the skin away when the tomatoes are cool enough to handle.

QUICK MEALS

*It is wonderful to spend time cooking long, leisurely meals,
but in reality, at the end of a busy day many of us don't have
that luxury. If you and your partner work hard during the
week, you will want food that is quick to prepare and on
the table in minutes. These recipes provide all the inspiration
you need to create fast, simple, delicious dishes when time is
short. They are much better for you than a takeaway and
ready in the same amount of time.*

500 g pasta, dried, fresh or stuffed, freshly cooked

3 tablespoons freshly grated Parmesan cheese, plus extra to serve

a handful of fresh herbs, torn or finely chopped, to serve (optional)

tomato sauce

1 kg canned plum tomatoes, drained (reserve the juice), deseeded and chopped

5 tablespoons extra virgin olive oil, plus extra to serve

4 garlic cloves

your choice of:
1 small piece of fresh chilli, ½ cinnamon stick, ½ teaspoon dried oregano or a bunch of fresh herbs such as basil

sea salt and freshly ground black pepper

serves 4-6

This classic tomato sauce comes originally from Campania, the region around Naples. It is made simply with tomatoes, olive oil, garlic and the flavouring of your choice.

quick neapolitan tomato sauce

To make the tomato sauce, put the prepared tomatoes, oil and garlic in a heavy-based saucepan. Add your choice of the chilli, cinnamon and dried or fresh herbs. Cover and simmer over low heat for 30 minutes, or until the tomatoes are reduced to a creamy mass. Stir from time to time to stop the sauce sticking to the bottom of the pan. Add a little of the reserved tomato juice whenever necessary to keep the sauce moist.

Discard the garlic and chilli, cinnamon or any woody herb stems and mash the sauce with a potato masher. If you prefer a smooth sauce, pass it through a blender. Season to taste with salt and freshly ground black pepper.

Pour the sauce over the freshly cooked pasta, top with the Parmesan and stir well. Transfer to a serving dish, sprinkle with fresh herbs, if using, then serve at once with extra Parmesan and a drizzle of olive oil.

penne *with mozzarella*

Bring a large saucepan of water to the boil, then add a large pinch of salt. Add the penne and cook until *al dente*, about 8 minutes.

Meanwhile, to make the sauce, put the tomatoes in a large, shallow saucepan or frying pan. Add the chilli, garlic, onion, tomato purée, oregano, sugar, balsamic vinegar, if using, and capers or olives. Cook, stirring, over high heat until the sauce is thick and reduced by about half. Add salt and pepper to taste.

Drain the pasta, reserving 3 tablespoons of the cooking liquid, then return the pasta and reserved liquid to the saucepan. Add the sliced mozzarella, pour the hot sauce over the top and toss and stir until well mixed and the mozzarella is softened and melting. Sprinkle with the olive oil and serve topped with basil sprigs.

Variation This dish can be made in advance. Cook the pasta and make the sauce as in the main recipe. Pour both into an ovenproof dish, but do not add the cheese. When ready to cook, bake in a preheated oven at 180°C (350°F) Gas 4 for 25–35 minutes or until very hot, bubbling and fragrant. Add the cheese and drizzle the oil on top. Bake for 2 minutes more until the cheese melts, then serve.

400 g penne rigate

400 g canned chopped plum tomatoes

1 small dried red chilli

3–4 garlic cloves, chopped

1 onion, chopped

2 tablespoons tomato purée

leaves from 2 sprigs of oregano or rosemary, chopped or torn

1 tablespoon sugar

1 tablespoon balsamic vinegar (optional)

50 g capers, or black olives, rinsed and drained (optional)

sea salt and freshly ground black pepper

to serve

150 g mozzarella cheese, sliced thinly, or torn into shreds

2 tablespoons extra virgin olive oil

sprigs of basil

serves 4

greek omelette

100 g cherry tomatoes, halved

4–5 bottled golden hot peppers, drained and sliced (the kind that come with kebabs)

3 spring onions, sliced

40 g pitted black olives, sliced

100 g feta cheese

a small handful of fresh flat leaf parsley, chopped

6 large free-range eggs

fine sea salt and freshly ground black pepper

extra virgin olive oil, for oiling the pan

crusty bread or pita, to serve (optional)

salad

200 g mixed leaves, washed and dried

1 tablespoon freshly squeezed lemon juice (a little less than ½ lemon)

4 tablespoons extra virgin olive oil

a metal pie plate or a deep ovenproof frying pan, rubbed with olive oil

serves 4 as a starter: 2 as a main course

This is not a traditional recipe. It's called a Greek omelette because all the ingredients are inspired by Greek cuisine. It is fast to make, nice to look at and easy to eat. Serve hot or cold, with crusty bread or pita.

Arrange the tomatoes, hot peppers, spring onions and olives equally around the oiled pan or pie plate. Crumble in the feta, then grind black pepper over the top. Sprinkle with parsley.

Put the eggs in a bowl, beat well and season with a good pinch of salt. Pour the eggs over the ingredients in the pan. Bake in a preheated oven at 200°C (400°F) Gas 6 until puffed and just golden around the edges, 15–20 minutes.

To make the salad, put the leaves in a bowl, add the lemon juice, oil, salt and pepper. Toss well, taste and adjust the seasoning with more salt and pepper, if necessary.

Serve the omelette – hot, warm or at room temperature – cut into wedges and accompanied by the salad and bread, if using.

risotto primavera

1 litre chicken or Vegetable Stock (see page 178)

100 g butter

3 tablespoons olive oil

1 onion, finely chopped

1 garlic clove, chopped

275 g arborio or carnaroli rice

625 g mixed green vegetables, such as asparagus, broad beans, dwarf beans, flat beans, runner beans, green cabbage, peas or spinach, all chopped into even-sized pieces

75 ml dry vermouth or white wine

a bunch of flat leaf parsley, chopped

125 g Parmesan cheese, freshly grated

sea salt and freshly ground black pepper

serves 4

Pour the stock into a small saucepan and heat to simmering point.

Heat the butter and olive oil in a large saucepan. Add the onion and garlic and cook over low heat for 5 minutes until softened and translucent, but not browned. Add the rice, stirring with a wooden spoon to coat the grains thoroughly with butter and oil.

Add a ladle of hot stock to the rice, mix well and let simmer. When the liquid has almost been absorbed by the rice, add another ladle of stock to the saucepan and stir constantly until it is absorbed. Continue, stirring the risotto and adding more stock as needed.

After the risotto has been cooking for 12 minutes, add all the vegetables and stir well. Add the remaining stock, vermouth or white wine, salt and pepper. Cook, stirring, for a further 4–5 minutes, then mix in the chopped parsley and grated Parmesan cheese. Cover and let rest for a couple of minutes, then serve.

moroccan prawns *with couscous*

4 tablespoons extra virgin olive oil

2 teaspoons ground cumin

1 teaspoon ground ginger

1 teaspoon paprika

½ teaspoon cayenne pepper

1 kg medium uncooked prawns, peeled

2 garlic cloves, crushed

2 lemons, 1 juiced, 1 cut into wedges

a bunch of coriander, leaves finely chopped

coarse sea salt and freshly ground black pepper

couscous

250 g instant couscous

½ teaspoon fine sea salt

3–4 tablespoons extra virgin olive oil

freshly squeezed juice of ½ lemon

serves 4

Instant couscous couldn't be simpler or faster to prepare. The prawns are a nicely spiced, quick little number to put on top, easily made in advance.

To prepare the couscous, put it in a large heatproof bowl, add ½ teaspoon salt and mix. Add 400 ml boiling water and 1 tablespoon oil. Cover and set aside for 5 minutes. Meanwhile, bring some water to the boil in the bottom of a steamer. Transfer the couscous to the top compartment of the steamer, cover and steam for 6–7 minutes. Fluff up with a fork and set aside.

Heat the oil in a sauté pan. Add the cumin, ginger, paprika and cayenne and cook, stirring, for 30 seconds. Add the prawns, garlic and a good pinch of salt. Cook, stirring, for 1 minute. Squeeze in the juice of 1 lemon and add 250 ml water. Stir, then cover and simmer until the prawns are opaque and cooked through, 3–5 minutes. Remove the pan from the heat and stir in the coriander. Taste and adjust the seasoning with salt, pepper and extra lemon juice if necessary.

Transfer the couscous to a serving plate. Season with the juice of ½ lemon and sprinkle with 2–3 tablespoons olive oil. Stir well. Put the prawns on top, pour over their cooking juices and serve with the lemon wedges.

green thai vegetable curry

This is a super-quick dish – it cooks just long enough for the vegetables to become tender.

Put the curry paste in a wok, heat and cook for 2 minutes, stirring. Add the coconut milk, stock and potato. Bring to the boil, reduce the heat and simmer for 5 minutes. Add the broccoli and cauliflower florets, stalk end down, cover with a lid and simmer for 4 minutes. Add the petit pois and sugar snap peas and cook for a further 2 minutes until all the vegetables are tender.

Ladle the curry into 4 bowls and serve with lime wedges and Thai fragrant rice.

3 tablespoons green Thai curry paste

400 ml canned coconut milk

425 ml Vegetable Stock (see page 178)

1 large potato, peeled and cut into 2.5 cm pieces

250 g broccoli florets

250 g cauliflower florets

125 g frozen petit pois

125 g sugar snap peas, halved lengthways

to serve

1 lime, cut into wedges

cooked Thai fragrant rice

serves 4

1 large fennel bulb, with leafy tops

2 tablespoons olive oil

2 garlic cloves, crushed

200 ml dry white wine

300 ml fish stock

800 g canned chopped tomatoes

a pinch of sugar

250 g cherry tomatoes, halved

500 g monkfish fillet, cut into 4 cm chunks

12 mussels, cleaned*

12 large, unpeeled, uncooked prawns, heads removed

sea salt and freshly ground black pepper

to serve

extra virgin olive oil

crusty bread (optional)

serves 4

Prawn shells are full of flavour, which seeps into the sauce and contributes to its richness. Eat this dish with your fingers and mop up with plenty of crusty bread.

mediterranean fish stew

Remove the leafy tops from the fennel bulb, chop them coarsely and set aside. Cut the bulb into quarters, remove and discard the core, then finely chop the bulb.

Heat the oil in a large saucepan or wok. Add the fennel bulb and fry for 5 minutes. Add the garlic and fry for a further 1 minute. Add the wine, stock, canned tomatoes and sugar and stir well. Bring to the boil, reduce the heat and simmer for 5 minutes. Add the cherry tomatoes and cook for 5 minutes more. Add lots of salt and pepper.

Add the monkfish and return to a simmer. Stir in the mussels and prawns, cover and cook for about 5 minutes, or until the mussels have opened and the fish is cooked. Ladle the stew into deep plates or bowls. Sprinkle with the fennel tops and olive oil and serve with crusty bread, if using.

*Note To clean the mussels, scrub them and rinse in several changes of cold water. Pull off the beards or seaweed-like threads and discard any mussels that don't close when tapped against the kitchen counter – these are dead and inedible.

---

50 g butter

2 leeks, thinly sliced

100 g smoked bacon, chopped

600 ml fish stock

125 g canned sweetcorn, drained and rinsed

100 g potatoes, peeled and cut into small cubes

300 g undyed smoked haddock fillets, skinned

1 tablespoon chopped fresh flat leaf parsley

1 tablespoon chopped fresh chives

100 ml double cream

sea salt and freshly ground black pepper

thick slices of mixed-grain bread, to serve

serves 8

smoked haddock chowder

This classic recipe is just perfect for damp and cold days – it is both warm and satisfying. In the US, they serve it with crumbled crackers, but you can serve it with mixed-grain bread.

Heat the butter in a large saucepan. Add the leeks and bacon and cook for 5 minutes, but do not brown. Add the fish stock and bring to a simmer. Add the sweetcorn, potatoes and fish and cook for 10 minutes. Add salt and pepper to taste and bring to a gentle boil.

Just before serving, stir in the parsley, chives and cream. Serve with thick slices of bread.

Watch the fillets carefully while cooking – they can easily overcook. Brushing the bars of the grill with a little oil will prevent the salmon from sticking.

barbecued salmon fillets
with basil & parmesan butter

6 fresh salmon fillets

steamed seasonal vegetables, to serve (optional)

basil and parmesan butter

175 g unsalted butter, softened

25 g freshly grated Parmesan cheese

1 teaspoon balsamic or sherry vinegar

25 g fresh basil leaves, sliced

freshly ground black pepper

marinade

1 large garlic clove, crushed

150 ml light olive oil

2 tablespoons balsamic or sherry vinegar

1–2 sprigs of thyme, crushed

serves 6

To make the basil and Parmesan butter, put the butter, Parmesan, vinegar, basil leaves and black pepper, to taste, in a bowl and beat well. Scoop onto to a piece of wet greaseproof paper and roll into a cylinder. Wrap in clingfilm and refrigerate (or freeze) for at least 1 hour, or until firm.

Put all the marinade ingredients in a wide, shallow dish, mix well, then add the salmon fillets and turn to coat well. Cover and let marinate for 20–30 minutes. Remove the fillets from the marinade and pat dry with kitchen paper.

Heat a barbecue until the coals are MEDIUM hot and white (no longer red). Lightly oil the grill bars, add the salmon and barbecue for about 3 minutes on each side until crisp and brown on the outside and just opaque all the way through – don't overcook it or the salmon will be dry. Alternatively, cook the salmon on a preheated stove-top grill pan. Serve the salmon fillets topped with slices of the chilled butter and with steamed seasonal vegetables, if using.

shrimp fried rice

This is a quick and easy dish to put together when you want something delicious but are short of time.

Heat the oil in a wok and swirl to coat. Add the garlic, ginger and chilli and stir-fry for 30 seconds. Add the prawns, peas, spring onions and dried shrimp and fry for 2 minutes until the prawns turn pink.

Using a spatula, push the mixture to one side. Add the eggs to the wok and scramble until set. Add the rice and stir over high heat for 2 minutes until heated through.

Stir in the soy sauce, lemon juice and coriander and serve.

*Note Packets of dried shrimp are available in Chinese or South-east Asian stores. They keep very well, even after opening.

2 tablespoons sunflower oil

2 garlic cloves, chopped

3 cm fresh ginger, peeled and grated

1 red chilli, deseeded and chopped

350 g small uncooked prawns, peeled, deveined and coarsely chopped

250 g frozen peas, thawed

6 spring onions, trimmed and sliced

4 tablespoons Asian dried shrimp*

2 eggs, lightly beaten

800 g cooked Thai fragrant rice (from 350 g uncooked rice)

3 tablespoons light soy sauce

freshly squeezed juice of ½ lemon

2 tablespoons chopped fresh coriander

serves 4

chicken 'panini' *with mozzarella*

250 g mozzarella cheese

4 large boneless, skinless chicken breasts

8 large fresh basil leaves, plus extra, to serve

2 garlic cloves, thinly sliced

1 tablespoon olive oil

sea salt and freshly ground black pepper

to serve

Salsa Rossa (see page 133)

mixed salad leaves

cocktail sticks

serves 4

Cut the mozzarella into 8 thick slices and set aside.

Put the chicken breasts on a board and, using a sharp knife, cut horizontally through the breast without cutting all the way through. Open out flat and season the insides with a little salt and pepper.

Put 2 basil leaves, a few garlic slices and 2 slices of cheese in each breast, then fold back over, pressing firmly together. Secure with cocktail sticks.

Brush the parcels with a little oil and cook on a preheated barbecue or stove-top grill pan for about 8 minutes on each side until the chicken is cooked and the cheese is beginning to ooze at the sides. Serve hot with the salsa rossa, a few basil leaves and mixed salad leaves.

Chicken is excellent poached in stock – the result is rich but healthy. Keep the leftover stock in this recipe to use another time.

wholegrain mustard tarragon chicken

Strip the tarragon leaves from the stalks, reserve the leaves and put the stalks in a large saucepan. Add the stock and cover the pan with a lid. Bring to the boil, then remove the lid and reduce the heat to a very gentle simmer, so the stock is barely moving.

Put the chicken breasts between 2 pieces of clingfilm and, using a rolling pin, flatten each piece to 1 cm thickness. Remove and discard the clingfilm.

Put the flattened chicken breasts in the stock and poach gently for about 15 minutes until firm to the touch and cooked through, with no trace of pink in the middle. Drain, reserving the stock for another recipe, and let the chicken cool a little. (The stock can be kept in the refrigerator for up to 3 days or frozen for up to 1 month.)

Meanwhile, coarsely chop the tarragon leaves and put them in a mini-blender. Add all the dressing ingredients and 1 teaspoon water and blend until smooth.

Slice the chicken diagonally into thin strips. Divide the salad leaves among 4 large plates and top with the slices of chicken. Drizzle with the dressing and serve immediately with crusty bread.

4 large sprigs of tarragon

2 litres chicken or Vegetable Stock (see page 178)

4 boneless, skinless chicken breasts

125 g salad leaves

crusty bread, to serve

mustard dressing

4 tablespoons extra virgin olive oil

1 teaspoon wholegrain mustard

sea salt and freshly ground black pepper

serves 4

parma-wrapped pork fillet
with spinach & lentil salad

2 pork fillets, 350 g each

8 thin slices of Parma ham

12 large fresh sage leaves, plus
1 tablespoon chopped fresh sage leaves

3 tablespoons extra virgin olive oil

4 shallots, finely chopped

1 garlic clove, crushed

800 g canned lentils, drained

100 ml chicken stock

freshly squeezed juice of ½ lemon

125 g baby spinach leaves

sea salt and freshly ground black pepper

serves 4

Pork can easily become dry. The solution is not to cook it at too high a heat, and in this recipe the sage and Parma ham wrapping help to keep it moist, while adding flavour.

Cut the pork fillets in half crossways to make 4 servings. Season with salt and pepper. Put 2 slices of Parma ham on a work surface, overlapping them slightly. Add 3 of the sage leaves in a line down the middle. Put a pork fillet on top and roll up, keeping the join underneath. Repeat with the remaining fillets.

Heat half the oil in a frying pan, add the pork fillets seam side down and fry over medium heat for 12–15 minutes, turning frequently until evenly browned. Transfer to a warm oven and let rest for 5 minutes.

Meanwhile, add the remaining oil to the pan, add the shallots, garlic and the chopped sage and fry for 3 minutes until softened but not golden. Add the lentils, chicken stock and lemon juice and heat through for 2–3 minutes. Stir in the spinach, cook until just wilted, then serve immediately with the pork.

1 tablespoon cumin seeds

1 tablespoon coriander seeds

1 tablespoon cracked black pepper

4 tablespoons fresh flat leaf
parsley, coarsely chopped

4 lamb steaks, from the leg,
about 150 g each

1 tablespoon olive oil

200 g Greek yoghurt

3 tablespoons chopped fresh
mint leaves

1 teaspoon freshly squeezed
lemon juice

sea salt and freshly ground
black pepper

a stove-top grill pan

serves 4

Lamb can throw off quite a bit of fat as it cooks. The grill pan keeps the meat out of the fat, which you can just pour off as it accumulates.

lamb steaks *with coriander cumin crust*

Crush the cumin and coriander seeds coarsely with a mortar and pestle or the back of a wooden spoon. Add the black pepper and parsley and stir to mix. Rub the lamb steaks with the olive oil and coat each side with the parsley and spice mixture.

Heat a stove-top grill pan until hot, add the lamb and cook for 2–3 minutes on each side for rare or 4–5 minutes for medium, depending on thickness.

While the lamb is cooking, put the yoghurt, mint and lemon juice in bowl, add salt and pepper to taste and mix well. Carve the grilled steaks into thick slices and serve with the minted yoghurt.

linguine *with peas, pancetta & sage*

300 g peas, fresh or frozen and defrosted

4–5 tablespoons extra virgin olive oil

5 tablespoons fresh breadcrumbs

500 g linguine

90 g thinly sliced pancetta, chopped

3 garlic cloves, crushed

a few sprigs of sage, leaves finely chopped

5 tablespoons dry white wine

25 g freshly grated Parmesan cheese

a small handful of fresh flat leaf parsley, chopped

fine sea salt and freshly ground black pepper

serves 4–6

Lightly blanch the peas in a saucepan of boiling water for 2–3 minutes. Drain and set aside.

Heat 2 tablespoons of the oil in a frying pan. Add the breadcrumbs and cook until golden, stirring occasionally, about 3 minutes. Season lightly with salt and pepper and set aside.

Cook the pasta in a large saucepan of boiling, salted water until *al dente*, or according to the packet instructions.

Heat 1 tablespoon of the remaining oil in a saucepan large enough to hold all the pasta later. Add the pancetta and cook, stirring, until browned, about 2 minutes. Add the garlic and cook, stirring, for 1 minute; don't let the garlic burn. Stir in the sage and wine. Cook, stirring, until the liquid has almost evaporated, about 1 minute. Set aside until needed.

Drain the cooked pasta thoroughly and add to the pan of pancetta. Add the peas and 1–2 tablespoons oil and cook over low heat, tossing well to mix. Stir in the cheese, parsley and pepper; taste and add more salt and pepper, if necessary. Sprinkle with the toasted breadcrumbs and serve hot.

peppered sage pork *with pasta*

2 sun-dried peppers

500 g pork fillet, sliced diagonally into 8 pieces

8 fresh sage leaves, plus 1 tablespoon chopped fresh sage leaves

250 g pappardelle or tagliatelle

15 g butter

½ tablespoon olive oil

50 ml dry sherry

200 ml double cream

100 ml chicken stock

sea salt and freshly ground black pepper

serves 4

Soak the sun-dried peppers in boiling water according to the instructions on the packet. Drain and cut into about 5 cm pieces.

Using the palm of your hand, gently flatten the pieces of pork into round medallion shapes. Using a small, sharp knife, make 2 small slits through the centre of each medallion. Thread a piece of sliced pepper through 1 slit and a sage leaf through the second slit of each medallion. Sprinkle with black pepper.

Cook the pasta in a large saucepan of boiling, salted water until *al dente*, or according to the packet instructions.

Meanwhile, heat the butter and oil in a non-stick frying pan until foaming. Add the pork medallions and fry over medium heat for 4–5 minutes on each side until golden and cooked through. Transfer to a warm plate, cover and set aside.

Pour the sherry into the hot frying pan and boil for 30 seconds. Stir in the cream, stock and chopped sage. Bring to the boil again, reduce the heat and simmer for 3–4 minutes. Add salt and pepper, to taste.

Drain the pasta, return it to the warm pan and toss with half of the cream sauce. Divide among 4 serving plates. Top each serving with 2 pieces of pork and pour over the remaining sauce. Serve immediately.

CLASSIC DISHES

There are certain dishes that every cook should have in his or her culinary repertoire. These classics are perfect for any occasion, whether you want something comforting for just the two of you or a tried and tested dish for a number of guests. Chilli with all the Trimmings is the answer if you are entertaining a large group, while Pizza is a welcome homemade treat for two.

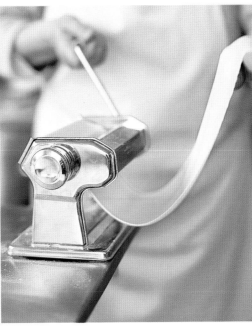

This meat sauce served with pasta is an all-time favourite. To make life easier, prepare double the quantity of sauce given here and freeze half for another time.

ragù

Heat the oil and butter in a heavy-based saucepan over medium heat. Add the carrot, celery, onion and pancetta and cook until the onion is translucent. Increase the heat, add the meat and fry until browned. Add the wine and let it bubble until it has evaporated.

Lower the heat, add enough milk to cover the meat, then add the tomato purée and nutmeg. Simmer rapidly until the milk has reduced by at least half. Lower the heat, top up with enough warm stock or water to cover the meat, stir, cover with a lid and simmer gently for at least 1 hour. Stir from time to time.

Add salt and pepper to taste, then cover and set aside to rest overnight to develop the flavours.

When ready to serve, reheat the sauce and add to the freshly cooked pasta. Stir in the Parmesan, parsley and the 25 g butter and serve with extra Parmesan sprinkled over the top.

500 g long or short egg pasta
or rigatoni, freshly cooked

ragù sauce

1 tablespoon olive oil

25 g unsalted butter

1 small carrot, finely chopped

1 small celery stalk, finely chopped

1 small onion, finely chopped

100 g pancetta or streaky bacon, minced

500 g lean minced steak

2 tablespoons white wine

375 ml full-fat milk, or enough to cover the meat

1½ tablespoons tomato purée

½ nutmeg, freshly grated

250–500 ml warm Vegetable Stock (see page 178) or water

sea salt and freshly ground black pepper

to serve

50 g freshly grated Parmesan cheese, plus extra to taste

3 tablespoons chopped fresh flat leaf parsley

25 g unsalted butter

serves 4-6

500 g pasta, such as spaghetti or penne, freshly cooked

carbonara sauce

2 whole free-range eggs

5 free-range egg yolks
(to separate eggs, see page 147)

25 g unsalted butter

125 ml single cream

6 tablespoons freshly grated Parmesan cheese, plus extra to serve

200 g pancetta or streaky bacon

olive oil, for frying

1 garlic clove, crushed

freshly ground black pepper

serves 4-6

carbonara

Crisp, garlic-scented bacon with a stream of creamy fresh eggs setting in warm pasta – an Italian classic.

Put the eggs and egg yolks in a bowl and mix lightly with a fork. Add the butter, cream, grated Parmesan and lots of black pepper. Let stand without mixing.

Chop the pancetta into slivers. Cover the base of a medium frying pan with olive oil and heat. When it starts to haze, add the pancetta. When the fat starts to run, add the crushed garlic and stir well. Continue frying until the pancetta becomes crisp and golden.

Add the pancetta and pan juices to the freshly cooked pasta and mix vigorously. Beat the egg mixture lightly with a fork and pour it over the pasta. Mix well and serve at once, sprinkled with extra Parmesan and plenty of black pepper – the butter will melt and the eggs will cook in the heat of the pasta.

tomato pizza
with capers & anchovies

If you are making fresh pizza bases, cook the pizzas one at a time and share them straight from the oven as soon as they are ready.

1 recipe Pizza Dough (see page 185),
2 packets pizza base mix (about 200 g each),
or 1 packet frozen pizza dough (500 g), halved

2 large ripe tomatoes, chopped

2 tablespoons capers, rinsed and drained

12 anchovy fillets in oil, drained and chopped

250 g buffalo mozzarella cheese, chopped

a few fresh basil leaves

sea salt and freshly ground black pepper

a pizza stone or baking sheet

serves 2

If using pizza base mix, prepare the dough according to the directions on the packet. Put the dough in a bowl and let rise until doubled in size.

Preheat the oven to its highest setting and put a pizza stone or baking sheet on the top shelf to heat.

Divide the risen dough in half and transfer one half to a well-floured work surface. Roll it out to 30 cm diameter. Take the hot stone or baking sheet from the oven and carefully put the pizza base on top.

Add half the tomatoes, half the capers, half the anchovies and half the mozzarella and top with a few basil leaves. Season with salt and pepper, to taste.

Bake in the preheated oven for 10–12 minutes until bubbling and golden. Serve at once, then repeat to make a second pizza.

rocket, bresaola & parmesan topping

3 plum tomatoes, sliced crossways

1 teaspoon caster sugar

extra virgin olive oil, for sprinkling

55 g rocket

8 slices bresaola, torn into pieces

55 g fresh Parmesan cheese shavings

sea salt and freshly ground black pepper

Make the pizza dough, divide it in half, then roll it out as in the main recipe, left. Arrange the tomato slices on top of the 2 pizza bases and sprinkle with the sugar, salt, pepper and olive oil. Bake, one at a time, as in the main recipe. Remove from the oven, top with half the rocket, half the bresaola and half the Parmesan. Sprinkle with oil and black pepper. Serve at once, then repeat to make a second pizza.

mozzarella, pine nuts, capers & basil topping

3 plum tomatoes, sliced crossways

1 teaspoon caster sugar

extra virgin olive oil, for sprinkling

175 g mozzarella cheese, preferably buffalo, sliced

55 g pine nuts, toasted

4 tablespoons baby capers, drained and rinsed

a large handful of basil leaves, torn

sea salt and freshly ground black pepper

Make the pizza dough, divide it in half, then roll it out as in the main recipe, left. Arrange the tomato slices on top of the 2 pizza bases and sprinkle with the sugar, salt, pepper and olive oil. Bake, one at a time, as in the main recipe. Remove from the oven, tear half of the mozzarella over the pizza, sprinkle with half the pine nuts and half the capers, then top with basil. Sprinkle with oil and black pepper. Serve at once, then repeat to make a second pizza.

There may seem a lot of mustard in this sauce, but, when you cook mustard, it loses its heat and you are left with a delicious flavour which no one can quite place once the poaching liquid has been added.

traditional fish pie

Put the milk in a wide saucepan, heat just to boiling point, then add the haddock. Turn off the heat and poach until opaque – do not overcook.

Meanwhile, melt 125 g of the butter in another saucepan, then stir in the mustard powder and flour. Remove the pan from the heat and strain the poaching liquid from the fish into the pan.

Arrange the fish and eggs in a shallow ovenproof dish or casserole.

Return the pan to the heat and, whisking vigorously to smooth out any lumps, bring the mixture to the boil. Season with salt and pepper, if necessary. (Take care: if you are using smoked fish, it may be salty enough.) Pour the sauce over the fish and eggs and mix carefully.

Cook the potatoes in boiling salted water until tender, then drain. Return to the pan. Melt the remaining butter in a small saucepan. Reserve 4 tablespoons of this butter and stir the remainder into the potatoes. Mash well and season with salt and pepper. Spoon the potatoes carefully over the sauced fish, then brush the surface of the potatoes generously with the reserved butter. Transfer the pie to a preheated oven at 200°C (400°F) Gas 6 for 20 minutes, or until nicely browned.

Note If smoked haddock is not available, add 125 g thinly sliced smoked salmon to the poached fish just before adding the sauce.

500 ml milk

750 g smoked or fresh haddock fillets, skinned

275 g unsalted butter

1 tablespoon dry English mustard powder

4 tablespoons plain flour

2 hard-boiled eggs, peeled and quartered

1 kg floury potatoes, peeled and cut into even-sized pieces

sea salt and freshly ground black pepper

a shallow ovenproof dish or casserole

serves 4

Cooking fish

- *It's important not to overcook fish – cook it just until it becomes opaque all the way through.*

- *Remember it keeps cooking after you remove it from the pan.*

- *Tuna can be served pink in the middle, but it must be very fresh. To make sure, buy it from a fishmonger.*

coq au vin

This modern version of the classic dish of chicken cooked in wine is a handy short cut. Cutting slashes in the chicken lets the marinade soak into and flavour the meat, while keeping it tender and moist.

4 boneless, skinless chicken breasts

150 ml red wine

1 garlic clove, sliced

2 tablespoons olive oil

a sprig of thyme, plus 4 sprigs to serve

sauce

20 g dried porcini mushrooms, rinsed thoroughly

1 tablespoon olive oil

6 shallots, halved

a pinch of sugar

125 g smoked bacon, chopped

1 garlic clove, crushed

2 teaspoons plain flour

150 ml red wine

150 ml port

a sprig of thyme

sea salt and freshly ground black pepper

a stove-top grill pan

serves 4

Using a small, sharp knife, slash the top of each chicken breast in a criss-cross fashion, taking care not to cut all the way through. Put the breasts in a shallow dish. Add the red wine, garlic, oil and a sprig of thyme and mix. Cover and refrigerate for 20 minutes. The chicken will absorb most of the marinade.

Meanwhile, to make the sauce, put the dried porcini in a heatproof bowl and cover with 150 ml boiling water. Let soak for 15 minutes, then drain, reserving the liquid. (The liquid can sometimes be gritty, so strain it through a tea strainer.) Coarsely chop the mushrooms.

Heat the oil in a frying pan. Add the shallots and sugar and fry for 10 minutes until golden. Add the bacon and garlic and fry for a further 5 minutes. Stir in the flour and cook for 1 minute. Add the mushrooms and their soaking liquid, red wine, port and a sprig of thyme. Bring to the boil, reduce the heat and simmer for 20 minutes until syrupy. Add salt and pepper to taste.

Meanwhile, heat a stove-top grill pan until hot. Transfer the chicken to the grill pan, discarding any remaining marinade. Cook for about 5 minutes on each side, until the chicken is cooked through, with no trace of pink in the middle. Serve the chicken with the sauce poured over and topped with the sprigs of thyme.

Chicken cooking tips

- *It's important to cook chicken all the way through. To test, push a skewer or small sharp knife into the thickest part. The juices that run out should be clear or golden — if they are pink or bloody, you must cook it for longer.*

- *To check whether chicken breasts are cooked, cut one to see. Cut through the thickest part — it should be opaque all the way through, with no trace of blood.*

- *Boneless, skinless chicken is quick and easy to cook, but if you cook it with the skin on and the bone in, it will have more flavour. Skin keeps it moist, while the bone helps conduct heat.*

tex-mex pork rack

2 racks barbecue pork spareribs,
500 g each

Chilli Spiked Cornbread, to serve
(see below)

sweet chilli marinade

2 garlic cloves, crushed

2 tablespoons sea salt

2 tablespoons ground cumin

2 teaspoons chilli powder

I teaspoon dried oregano

8 tablespoons maple syrup or
golden syrup

4 tablespoons red wine vinegar

4 tablespoons olive oil

serves 4-6

Nibbling away at succulent grilled pork ribs is one of the true pleasures of a barbecue and here they are cooked in a marinade of spices and maple syrup giving them the authentic flavour of the American deep south.

Wash the ribs and pat them dry with kitchen paper. Transfer to a shallow, non-metal dish.

Put all the marinade ingredients in a bowl and mix well. Pour it over the ribs, then work in well with your hands. Cover and let marinate overnight in the refrigerator.

The next day, return the ribs to room temperature for I hour, then cook on a preheated medium-hot barbecue for about 30 minutes, turning and basting frequently with the marinade juices. Let cool slightly, then serve with chilli spiked cornbread.

150 g medium cornmeal

150 g plain flour

1½ teaspoons salt

I tablespoon baking powder

2 eggs, beaten

250 ml milk

2 tablespoons olive oil

2 large red chillies, deseeded and chopped

200 g canned corn kernels, drained

25 g finely grated Cheddar cheese

2 tablespoons chopped fresh coriander

*a cake tin, 20 cm square, greased and
base-lined with baking parchment*

serves 8

chilli spiked cornbread

This is a great savoury bread, ideal for picnics. It is quick and easy to make and can be eaten as a snack or as part of a meal.

Put the cornmeal, flour, salt and baking powder in a bowl and mix. Make a well in the centre and pour in the eggs, milk and olive oil. Beat with a wooden spoon to make a smooth batter.

Fold in the chillies, corn, cheese and coriander, then spoon the mixture into the prepared cake tin. Bake in a preheated oven at 200°C (400°F) Gas 6 for 25 minutes, or until a skewer inserted in the centre comes out clean.

Remove from the oven and let cool in the tin for about 5 minutes, then turn out onto a wire rack to cool completely. Cut into squares to serve.

The combination of orange, tomato and chilli gives this dish a Spanish rather than Italian flavour, but the sauce is only lightly spiced, making it a good choice for younger guests (omit the cayenne altogether if you prefer). The sauce and/or meatballs can easily be made a day ahead; in fact, it's better that way. Serve with a red Rioja and roasted or sautéed potatoes. Any leftovers make a great sandwich filling, stuffed in a baguette, wrapped in foil and warmed in the oven.

meatballs in red pepper sauce

50 g fresh breadcrumbs

3 tablespoons milk

1 small onion, finely chopped

a handful of fresh flat leaf parsley, chopped

2 garlic cloves, finely chopped

800 g minced meat, preferably a mix of beef and pork

1½ teaspoons fine sea salt

1 teaspoon dried oregano

1 teaspoon ground cumin

½ teaspoon sweet smoked paprika

1 egg, beaten

3 tablespoons extra virgin olive oil

red pepper sauce

2 red peppers

2 tablespoons extra virgin olive oil, plus extra for rubbing

several sprigs of fresh thyme

1 bay leaf

1 onion, grated

6 garlic cloves, crushed

¼ teaspoon cayenne pepper (optional)

5 tablespoons red wine

½ unwaxed orange, well scrubbed

1 litre passata

sea salt and freshly ground black pepper

kitchen foil

a baking sheet

kitchen string

a baking dish (see method)

makes about 25 meatballs

To make the red pepper sauce, rub the peppers with olive oil, then put them on a sheet of foil on a baking sheet (make the piece of foil large enough to fold over and enclose the peppers after roasting). Roast in a preheated oven at 220°C (425°F) Gas 7 until tender and charred, 30–40 minutes. Remove from the oven, enclose in the foil and set aside to loosen the skin. When cool enough to handle, about 30 minutes, remove the skins and seeds, chop the flesh coarsely and set aside. Lower the oven temperature to 200°C (400°F) Gas 6.

Meanwhile, tie the thyme and bay leaf together with kitchen string. Heat 2 tablespoons of the oil in a frying pan. Add the onion and a pinch of salt and cook until soft, 2–3 minutes. Add the garlic and cayenne, if using, and cook, stirring, for 1 minute. Stir in the wine and squeeze in the orange juice (reserve the rest of the orange) and cook for 30 seconds. Add the passata, a good pinch of salt, the bunch of herbs and the reserved orange half. Simmer gently until thick, 20–30 minutes. Add salt and pepper to taste. Stir in the red peppers, remove and discard the herbs and orange and transfer to a baking dish large enough to hold the meatballs in a single layer. This sauce can be made a day ahead.

To make the meatballs, put the breadcrumbs, milk, onion, parsley, garlic, minced meat, salt, oregano, cumin, paprika and beaten egg in a large bowl. Mix well (your hands are best). Shape spoonfuls of the meat mixture into balls, just slightly larger than a golf ball. Set on a tray.

To cook, heat 3 tablespoons oil in a large, heavy frying pan. Working in batches, cook the meatballs until browned evenly, about 5 minutes per batch – don't worry if they don't stay perfectly formed. Using a slotted spoon, transfer the browned meatballs to the sauce in the baking dish. When all the meatballs are browned, gently spoon some sauce over each one, then cover the baking dish with foil and bake for 20 minutes in the preheated oven. Serve hot.

The classic version of this dish is pasta layered with meat sauce and creamy 'salsa besciamella'. It is very easy to assemble. Make the ragù the day before, and the besciamella sauce on the day. Just make sure the ragù is quite liquid. This will be absorbed into the pasta as it cooks. Vary the recipe by replacing the meat sauce with a mixture of ricotta, spinach, chopped sun-dried tomatoes, Parmesan and fresh herbs.

lasagne

about 12 sheets dried lasagne verdi

about 50 g freshly grated Parmesan cheese

besciamella sauce

150 g butter

110 g plain white flour

about 1 litre milk

sea salt

ragù

75 g pancetta or dry-cure smoked bacon in a piece

100 g chicken livers

50 g butter

1 medium onion, finely chopped

1 medium carrot, chopped

1 celery stick, trimmed and finely chopped

250 g lean minced beef

2 tablespoons tomato purée

100 ml dry white wine

200 ml beef stock or water

freshly grated nutmeg

sea salt and freshly ground black pepper

a deep baking dish, about 20 x 25 cm, buttered

serves 4-6

To make the besciamella, melt the butter in a medium saucepan. When foaming, add the flour and cook over gentle heat for about 5 minutes without letting it brown. Have a balloon whisk ready. Slide the pan off the heat and add all the milk at once, whisking very well. When all the flour and butter have been amalgamated and there are no lumps, return to the heat and slowly bring to the boil, whisking all the time. When it comes to the boil, add salt, simmer gently for 2–3 minutes, then use immediately.

If making in advance, cover the surface directly with clingfilm to prevent a skin forming, then let cool. When reheating, remove the clingfilm and reheat very gently, stirring every now and then until liquid. Don't worry too much about lumps – they will disappear when the whole dish cooks. If you like a thinner sauce, just add extra milk after it has boiled and thickened.

To make the ragù, cut the pancetta into small cubes. Trim the chicken livers, removing any fat or gristle. Cut off any discoloured bits, which will be bitter if left on. Coarsely chop the livers.

Melt the butter in a saucepan, add the pancetta and cook for 2–3 minutes until browning. Add the onion, carrot and celery and brown these too. Stir in the minced beef and brown until just changing colour, but not hardening – break it up with a wooden spoon. Stir in the chicken livers and cook for 2–3 minutes. Add the tomato purée, mix well and pour in the wine and stock. Season well with nutmeg, salt and pepper. Bring to the boil, cover and simmer very gently for as long as you can – 2 hours if possible.

Cook the sheets of dried lasagne in plenty of boiling water in batches according to the packet instructions. Lift out with a slotted spoon and drain on a clean tea towel.

Spoon one-third of the meat sauce into a buttered baking dish. Cover with 4 sheets of lasagne and spread with one-third of the besciamella. Repeat the layers twice more, finishing with a layer of besciamella covering the whole top. Sprinkle with Parmesan cheese. Bake in a preheated oven at 180°C (350°F) Gas 4 for about 45 minutes until brown and bubbling. Let stand for 10 minutes to settle and firm up before serving.

Forget the stuff that's slopped on jacket potatoes – this is the real thing, made with finely chopped chuck steak instead of mince and spiced with several types of chilli, not the ubiquitous chilli powder from the supermarket shelf. That said, maybe Texas cowboys didn't put red wine in their chilli, but surely they'd approve of the addition. The various bits to put on at the end are also fairly urban, but they fill out the table nicely and add to the enjoyment.

chilli *with all the trimmings*

Put the chipotle in a small heatproof bowl and just cover with hot water. Let soak for at least 15 minutes, or as long as it takes to prepare all the other ingredients.

Heat 2 tablespoons of the oil in a large saucepan. Add the peppers, onion, celery, green chilli and a good pinch of salt and cook until soft, 5–7 minutes, stirring frequently. Remove from the pan and set aside. Increase the heat under the pan, add the remaining 2 tablespoons of the oil and the steak. Cook, stirring frequently until browned, 1–2 minutes. Add the garlic and another pinch of salt and cook, stirring constantly for 1 minute. Add the wine, bring to the boil and cook for 1 minute.

Return the pepper and onion mixture to the pan and stir in the chilli flakes, cumin and oregano. Add the tomatoes, beans, bay leaf and a good pinch of salt and stir well. Remove the chipotle from the soaking liquid, chop finely and stir into the pan, along with the soaking liquid. Cover and simmer gently until the meat is tender, 15–20 minutes. Add salt and pepper to taste.

At this point, the chilli is ready, but you should set it aside for at least 2–3 hours before serving to develop the flavours or, ideally, make it 1 day in advance and chill until needed. When ready to serve, remove the bay leaf, reheat the chilli and serve hot, with all the trimmings in separate bowls.

1 chipotle chilli (dried smoked jalapeño)*

4 tablespoons extra virgin olive oil

4 peppers (1 red, 1 yellow, 1 orange, 1 green), halved, deseeded and chopped

1 large onion

2 celery sticks, chopped

½–1 green chilli, finely chopped

800 g chuck steak, cut into small cubes

3 garlic cloves, chopped

250 ml red wine, fresh beef stock or water

¼ teaspoon dried chilli flakes

2 teaspoons ground cumin

2 teaspoons dried oregano

800 g canned chopped peeled tomatoes

1.2 kg canned red kidney beans (3 cans), drained and rinsed

1 bay leaf

coarse sea salt and freshly ground black pepper

to serve

1–2 ripe avocados, chopped and tossed with lime juice

a bunch of spring onions, chopped

a bunch of coriander, chopped

8–12 tortillas (at least 2 per person), warmed

sour cream or crème fraîche

freshly grated cheese, such as mild Cheddar or Double Gloucester

lime wedges

Tabasco sauce

serves 6-8

If you are unable to find chipotles in a delicatessen, The Cool Chile Company supplies them by mail order. Visit www.coolchile.co.uk.

These wedges have a delicious spice mix coating that makes them the ideal partner for steak or simple roasts. Even better, add some crushed garlic to a bowl of mayonnaise and use as a dip.

potato wedges
with garlic & paprika

1.5 kg potatoes, unpeeled but well scrubbed

1 bay leaf

5 tablespoons extra virgin olive oil

3 garlic cloves, finely chopped

1 tablespoon dried oregano

1 teaspoon sweet smoked Spanish paprika

a handful of fresh flat leaf parsley, chopped

coarse sea salt and freshly ground black pepper

a baking sheet

serves 4

If the potatoes are large, cut in half lengthways, otherwise leave them whole. Put them in a large saucepan of water with the bay leaf and 1 heaped tablespoon of coarse sea salt. Bring the water to the boil and cook the potatoes until just tender, but not completely soft. Drain and let cool slightly.

When the potatoes are cool enough to handle, cut into wedges. Put in a large dish and add the oil, garlic, oregano, paprika and salt and mix well with your hands until evenly coated.

Arrange the wedges in a single layer on a baking sheet and bake in a preheated oven at 230°C (450°F) Gas 8 until browned, 30–40 minutes. Sprinkle with pepper and parsley and serve hot.

french fries

500 g floury potatoes (for baking and frying)

sunflower oil, for frying

sea salt

a large saucepan with frying basket, or an electric deep-fryer

serves 4

Peel the potatoes and cut into 5 mm slices. Cut the slices into 5 mm strips. Put the strips in a bowl of iced water and leave for at least 5 minutes. When ready to cook, drain well and pat dry with kitchen paper.

Fill a large saucepan one-third full with oil, or if using a deep-fryer to the manufacturer's recommended level. Heat the oil to 190°C (375°F) or until a cube of bread will brown in 30 seconds. Working in batches, put 2 large handfuls of potato strips in the frying basket, lower carefully into the oil and fry for about 4 minutes. Remove and drain on kitchen paper. Repeat until all the strips have been cooked.

Skim any debris off the top of the oil, reheat the oil to 190°C (375°F), then fry the strips, in batches, for a second time until crisp and golden, about 2 minutes. Remove and drain on kitchen paper, then sprinkle with salt. Serve immediately.

This French classic is a much more sophisticated version of macaroni cheese. It is ideal for serving with beef stews, as the gratin is even better when mixed with broth.

macaroni gratin

300 g thin macaroni

500 ml milk

3 tablespoons crème fraîche

60 g unsalted butter

4 tablespoons plain flour

200 g finely grated Beaufort cheese*

coarse sea salt and freshly
ground black pepper

a baking dish, 30 cm long, buttered

serves 6

Cook the macaroni in plenty of boiling, well-salted water according to the instructions on the packet. Drain and rinse well.

Heat the milk in the rinsed saucepan and stir in the crème fraîche. Melt the butter in a second saucepan over medium-high heat. Stir in the flour and cook, stirring constantly, for 3 minutes. Pour in the milk mixture and stir constantly until the mixture thickens. Season with salt and pepper.

Stir the macaroni into the milk mixture and taste, adding salt and pepper if necessary. Transfer to the prepared baking dish and sprinkle with the cheese. Cook under a preheated grill until bubbling and browned, 10–15 minutes. Serve hot.

*Note Beaufort is an Alpine cheese, similar to Gruyère, but with a slightly sweeter, more pronounced nutty flavour. It is becoming more widely available outside France, but if you cannot find it, Emmental, Cantal or any firm, Cheddar-like cheese will do.

Choose large 'old' potatoes – the sort that become fluffy when mashed. When boiling potatoes, it's important to always add salt to the water before cooking.

classic creamy mashed potatoes

1 kg large 'old' potatoes, such as baking potatoes, peeled and cut into 5 cm cubes

about 150 ml milk, preferably hot

40 g butter

sea salt and freshly ground black pepper

serves 4

Put the potatoes in a medium saucepan. Cover with cold water and add a pinch of salt.

Bring to the boil, reduce the heat, half-cover with a lid and simmer for 15–20 minutes until tender when pierced with a knife. Drain and return the potatoes to the pan.

Return the saucepan to the heat and mash the potatoes with a fork or potato masher for 30 seconds – this will steam off any excess water.

Stir in the milk and butter, then mash until smooth, adding extra milk, if necessary. Season to taste with salt and pepper. Serve immediately.

Mashed potato tips

- *Best for mashing are large 'old' potatoes (often called floury or baking potatoes). They become light and fluffy when boiled.*

- *Cut them into even-sized pieces, so they will cook at the same rate and all be ready at the same time.*

- *Always start them in COLD water. Bring to the boil, then simmer – with the lid slightly ajar – until tender when pierced with the point of a knife.*

- *Never use a food processor to mash your potatoes – you'll end up with wallpaper glue.*

SPECIAL OCCASIONS

Forget the rushed meals during the week, on certain occasions you will want to prepare something extra-special for your loved one. Whether it's your anniversary, birthday or Valentine's Day, or simply because you want to give your partner a treat, here are some great ideas for you to try. Oysters make a romantic start to a meal for two. Follow these with Beef en Croûte and finish with a decadent dessert, such as Raspberries in Champagne Jelly from page 144.

seared scallops
with brittle parma

Scallops cook fast, and carry on cooking off the heat, so keep a careful watch on them – when overcooked, they are tough.

4 slices of Parma ham
12 large scallops
125 g salad leaves, such as lamb's lettuce
freshly ground black pepper

to drizzle
extra virgin olive oil
balsamic vinegar

a stove-top grill pan

serves 4

Heat a stove-top grill pan until very hot. Add the ham and cook for 1–2 minutes on each side until crisp. Remove from the pan and set aside.

Grind black pepper over the scallops, then add the scallops to the hot pan. Cook for 1–2 minutes on each side until they are opaque.

Divide the salad leaves among 4 serving plates. Lightly drizzle with oil and a little balsamic vinegar.

Top each serving of salad with 3 scallops, then break over the brittle Parma ham. Sprinkle with black pepper and serve at once.

oysters rockefeller

This adaptation of the classic dish – invented in New Orleans in the 1890s – makes a decadent starter when served with champagne.

1 shallot, finely chopped
1 small garlic clove, crushed
1 small piece of Florence fennel, finely chopped
75 g unsalted butter
90 ml double cream
3 sprigs of flat leaf parsley
4 sprigs of chervil
4 sprigs of watercress
2 teaspoons Pernod
24 oysters
a large pinch of cayenne pepper
6 tablespoons fresh breadcrumbs
6 tablespoons freshly grated Parmesan cheese
sea salt and freshly ground black pepper

a grill pan, lined with foil

serves 6

Put the shallot, garlic, fennel and butter in a frying pan, heat gently and cook until softened and translucent. Add the cream and simmer for 2 minutes. Remove from the heat. Remove the leaves from the parsley, chervil and watercress sprigs. Chop them and add to the pan along with the Pernod.

To shuck the oysters, hold them firmly in one hand (you can wrap that hand in a tea towel, for safety reasons, if you like). Insert a knife into the hinge of the shell and twist it until the top shell is loosened, then twist it off. Loosen the oysters from both sides of their shell with a knife and leave them in the deepest shell. Arrange the flat shells on the foil-lined grill pan and balance the round shells on top. Put 1 teaspoon of the herb mixture on top of each oyster.

Put the cayenne, breadcrumbs, Parmesan, salt and pepper in a bowl and stir well. Sprinkle 1 teaspoon of the mixture over each oyster. Cook under a preheated, very hot grill until just golden, 30–60 seconds. Serve immediately; the idea is not to cook the oysters but to maintain a hot-cold contrast.

This garlicky, saffron-scented sauce used here is a slightly
more flavoursome departure from the classic French mussel
recipe with shallots and white wine, called 'à la marinière'.

mussels *with fennel, tomatoes, garlic & saffron*

2 tablespoons extra virgin olive oil

1 small onion, chopped

½ fennel bulb, chopped

4 garlic cloves, crushed

250 ml dry white wine

400 g canned chopped tomatoes

a pinch of saffron threads

1 kg fresh mussels

coarse sea salt

a handful of fresh flat leaf parsley,
chopped, to serve

serves 4

Heat the oil in a large sauté pan. Add the onion and fennel and
cook until soft, 3–5 minutes. Add the garlic, wine and tomatoes.
Boil for 1 minute, then lower the heat, add the saffron and a pinch
of salt. Simmer gently for 15 minutes.

Just before serving, clean and debeard the mussels, discarding any
that do not close. (To clean mussels, see note on page 59.)

Raise the heat under the sauce and, when boiling, add the
prepared mussels. Cover and cook until the mussels open,
2–3 minutes. Discard any that do not open. Serve immediately,
sprinkled with parsley.

Variation French fries are the classic accompaniment for mussels
when served as a main course. See the recipe on page 87.

smoked wild salmon & scrambled eggs *with avruga*

Use caviar if you are wildly rich – and try the scrambled
eggs made with duck eggs. These are available from some
delicatessens and farm shops.

Break the eggs into a bowl and whisk lightly. Add the milk and whisk again.
Melt the butter in a non-stick saucepan, then add the eggs and salt and
pepper to taste. Cook, stirring constantly with a small wooden spoon, for
about 5–8 minutes until the eggs are softly scrambled. Remove the pan
from the heat just before the eggs are done, as they will continue to cook.

Warm the bread in a preheated oven at 180°C (350°F) Gas 4 for
10 minutes and put onto serving plates. Spoon the scrambled eggs onto
the toast and top with some smoked salmon. Add 1 teaspoon of avruga,
if using, and serve at once, topped with a few chives.

8 hen eggs or 4 duck eggs

100 ml milk

50 g butter

8 slices mixed-grain bread

250 g smoked wild salmon,
sliced

100 g avruga or salmon
caviar (optional)

sea salt and white pepper

a bunch of chives, to serve

serves 8

tuna *with paprika crumbs*

Tuna takes well to hot paprika seasoning. The topping gives a moist and crunchy texture to a fish that can become dry and overcooked only too easily.

To make the romesco sauce, char the peppers under a preheated hot grill, put them in a paper bag, seal and let steam for 10 minutes. Remove the skin, seeds and membranes. Heat 1 teaspoon of the oil in a non-stick pan, lightly brown the garlic, then add the chilli and tomatoes. Dry out the mixture over high heat so it starts to fry and even brown a little. Transfer to a blender, add the peppers, vinegar and remaining oil and purée until smooth. Stir in the nuts to thicken the sauce and add salt to taste.

To make the paprika topping, heat the oil in a frying pan, add the breadcrumbs, basil, paprika, tomato purée, sugar and ½ teaspoon salt. Stir well and fry until crunchy. Remove from the pan and let cool.

Season the tuna with salt and pepper, put on the oiled baking sheet and roast in a preheated oven at 250°C (500°F) Gas 9 for 5 minutes. Remove from the oven and turn the steaks over. Pile the paprika breadcrumbs on top, then add the slice of cheese, if using. Return to the oven and cook for a further 5 minutes or until the cheese has melted. Serve on a bed of buttered spinach or rocket salad, with romesco sauce served separately.

4 tuna steaks, 175 g each

40 g Cheddar cheese, cut into 4 thin slices (optional)

sea salt and freshly ground black pepper

buttered spinach or rocket salad, to serve

romesco sauce

2 red peppers

100 ml olive oil

2 garlic cloves

1 fresh red chilli, deseeded and sliced

200g canned plum tomatoes

25 ml red wine vinegar

1 tablespoon ground hazelnuts

1 tablespoon ground almonds

paprika breadcrumb crunch

1 tablespoon olive oil

50 g fresh white breadcrumbs

1 tablespoon chopped fresh basil leaves

½ teaspoon hot oak-smoked paprika

1 teaspoon tomato purée

½ teaspoon sugar

a baking sheet, oiled

serves 4

sole meunière

Put some flour on a large plate, add the fish, cover with flour on both sides and shake off the excess.

Reserve 2 tablespoons of the butter. Heat the oil and remaining butter over medium-high heat in a non-stick frying pan large enough to hold both fish side by side. When it sizzles, add the sole and cook for about 3 minutes. Turn them over and cook on the other side for 3 minutes. Sprinkle the first side with salt while the second side is cooking.

When the fish is cooked through, transfer to warmed serving plates and season the second side with salt.

Return the frying pan to the heat, add the remaining 2 tablespoons butter and melt over high heat. When it begins to sizzle, lower the heat and add the lemon juice. Cook, scraping the pan for about 10 seconds; do not let the butter burn. Pour this lemon butter over the fish and sprinkle with parsley. Serve immediately with lemon slices.

plain flour, for dusting

2 soles, about 300 g, skinned and cleaned

40 g unsalted butter

2 tablespoons sunflower oil

freshly squeezed juice of ½ lemon

fine sea salt

to serve

a handful of fresh flat leaf parsley, finely chopped

½ lemon, thinly sliced

serves 2

Serve these delicious duck breasts with sautéed or roasted potatoes and a good bottle of red wine.

duck breasts *with peppercorns*

2 French duck magrets or 4 duck breasts, about 650 g in total

3 tablespoons Cognac

200 ml crème fraîche

1 tablespoon coarsely ground black pepper

1 tablespoon green peppercorns in brine, drained

coarse sea salt

sautéed or roasted potatoes, to serve

serves 2

Trim the excess fat from around the duck breasts, then score the skin in a diamond pattern.

Heat a heavy frying pan. When hot, add the duck skin side down and cook for 7–8 minutes. Turn and cook the other side for 4–5 minutes, depending on thickness. Remove from the pan, season with salt and keep them warm.

Drain almost all the fat from the pan. Return to the heat and add the Cognac, scraping the bottom of the pan. Stir in the crème fraîche, black pepper and green peppercorns and cook for 1 minute.

Slice the duck diagonally lengthways and put on warm serving plates. Pour the sauce over the top and serve immediately with your choice of potatoes.

250 g mixed salad leaves, such as frisée, baby spinach or rocket

4 tablespoons extra virgin olive oil

750 g thin asparagus spears, 10–12 per person

4 boneless, skinless chicken breasts

100 g Gorgonzola cheese, cut into 4 slices

20 g shelled hazelnuts, coarsely crushed

fine sea salt and freshly ground black pepper

dressing

3 tablespoons freshly squeezed orange juice

1 teaspoon Dijon mustard

½ teaspoon fine sea salt

8 tablespoons extra virgin olive oil

baking parchment

a stove-top grill pan

serves 4

chicken, asparagus & gorgonzola salad *with hazelnuts*

To make the dressing, put the orange juice, mustard and salt in a small bowl and whisk until blended. Add the oil, a spoonful at a time, and whisk until thick. Season with pepper. Put the salad leaves in a bowl, add half the dressing and toss well. Divide the leaves among 4 serving plates and set aside.

Heat 2 tablespoons of the oil in a large, non-stick frying pan. Add half the asparagus and cook on high heat for 3 minutes without stirring (you want the asparagus to char). Season with salt and continue to cook for 1–2 minutes. Transfer to a dish and set aside. Repeat with the remaining asparagus. Top each mound of salad with some asparagus.

Put each chicken breast between 2 large sheets of baking parchment and pound until flattened. Rub the chicken breasts with olive oil and season with salt and pepper. To cook, heat a stove-top grill pan, add the chicken and cook for 2–3 minutes on each side until cooked through.

Put the chicken on top of the asparagus and top it with a slice of Gorgonzola. Sprinkle some hazelnuts and a spoonful of dressing over each serving, add a grinding of pepper and serve.

spicy-crust roasted rack of lamb

3 tablespoons cumin seeds

2 tablespoons coriander seeds

2 teaspoons black peppercorns

4 cloves

4 small dried chillies

2 tablespoons sea salt

grated zest and freshly squeezed juice of 2 unwaxed lemons

4 tablespoons olive oil

3 racks of lamb, 6 cutlets each

200 ml red wine

Mashed Minty Potatoes and Peas, to serve (see below)

serves 8

Heat a dry frying pan and add the cumin and coriander seeds, peppercorns, cloves and chillies. Cook for 1 minute, stirring frequently. Transfer to a mortar and crush coarsely with a pestle. Transfer to a bowl and stir in the salt, lemon zest and juice and oil.

Put the racks of lamb in a large roasting tin. Rub the spice mixture into the lamb, smearing well all over. Cover and chill in the refrigerator overnight.

Cook the lamb in a preheated oven at 200°C (400°F) Gas 6 for 20 minutes then reduce to 180°C (350°F) Gas 4. Cook for a further 20 minutes for rare meat, 25 minutes for medium and 35 minutes for well done. Remove from the oven, transfer to a carving board and let rest for 5 minutes in a warm place.

Meanwhile, add the wine and 200 ml water to the roasting tin and set it on top of the stove over high heat. Stir to scrape up all the roasted bits on the bottom of the tin, and boil until reduced by half.

Cut the lamb into separate cutlets and arrange on top of the mashed minty potatoes and peas. Spoon a little sauce over the top and serve.

This simple combination creates a two-in-one vegetable dish, making life in the kitchen a little easier. The mashed potato mixture can be prepared in advance, but don't add the mint until just before serving or it will lose its vibrant, fresh look.

mashed minty potatoes & peas

Cook the potatoes in a large saucepan of boiling, salted water for about 20 minutes, or until tender when pierced with a knife. Drain well and return them to the pan. Shake the pan a few times, then put over low heat for 2 minutes to steam off any excess moisture.

Add the butter, egg, milk, salt and pepper to the pan. Stir briefly, then remove from the heat and crush the potatoes briefly with the back of a wooden spoon. Keep the potatoes warm while you cook the peas.

Bring a saucepan of salted water to the boil, add the peas and cook for 2 minutes. Drain well, add to the potatoes, then add the mint. Mix gently, crushing the peas lightly into the potato, but keeping some whole.

1.5 kg floury potatoes, cut into even-sized pieces

50 g butter

1 egg, beaten

100 ml milk

300 g frozen baby peas

a bunch of mint, chopped

sea salt and freshly ground black pepper

serves 8

A summery way of enjoying roast beef without too much heat from the kitchen. Par-boiling the potatoes before roasting means that they won't dry out and shrivel as they roast.

seared peppered beef salad
with horseradish dressing

500 g baby new potatoes, unpeeled, par-boiled for 12–15 minutes (see box below), until nearly cooked through

2 tablespoons olive oil

250 g baby plum tomatoes

4 fillet steaks, 125 g each

1 tablespoon Worcestershire sauce

100 g wild rocket

125 g sugar snap peas, trimmed, blanched, refreshed (see below) and halved lengthways

sea salt and freshly ground black pepper

horseradish dressing

3 tablespoons crème fraîche

1–2 tablespoons creamed horseradish

a squeeze of fresh lemon juice

a stove-top grill pan

serves 4

Put the par-boiled potatoes in a roasting tin and toss with 1 tablespoon oil, to coat. Sprinkle with salt and black pepper, transfer to a preheated oven at 220°C (425°F) Gas 7 and roast for 25–30 minutes until browned and starting to crisp.

Remove from the oven and, using a large metal spoon, push the potatoes to one end of the tin, in a pile. Put the baby plum tomatoes into the empty half of the tin and sprinkle with 1 tablespoon olive oil, salt and pepper. Roast in the oven for 15 minutes until just soft.

Meanwhile, put all the dressing ingredients in a bowl and mix well. Add salt and pepper to taste.

Sprinkle the steaks with plenty of black pepper and drizzle with the Worcestershire sauce. Preheat a stove-top grill pan, add the beef and sear for 1–2 minutes on each side or until cooked to your liking. Set aside and let rest.

Put the rocket and sugar snap peas in a bowl and toss well. Divide among 4 serving plates. Spoon the potatoes and tomatoes around the rocket and peas.

Slice the beef diagonally and arrange the slices over the salad. Top with a dollop of horseradish dressing and serve, with any remaining dressing served separately.

Blanching, refreshing and par-boiling

- *'Blanching' means partially cooking foods, especially vegetables, by dunking them briefly in boiling water. This is especially good for green beans and broccoli, when you want a good, crunchy salad or if you are going to stir-fry the vegetables afterwards. Drain as soon as they turn a bright green, then refresh (see below).*

- *'Refreshing' is when the blanched food is plunged into iced water to stop it cooking and to set the colour. Drain again when it's cold.*

- *'Par-boiling' is when the foods, often vegetables, are half cooked by boiling in order to be finished by some other cooking method, often roasting. Par-boiling potatoes and parsnips before roasting them stops them drying out or shrivelling before they are roasted and cooked through.*

For added luxury, use a mixture of porcini and portobello mushrooms. Just make sure they are completely cold when you put them onto the pastry, and drain off any excess liquid.

beef en croûte

4 tablespoons olive oil

3 shallots, finely chopped

2 garlic cloves, chopped

150 g portobello mushrooms, sliced

1.25 kg fillet of beef, trimmed

500 g puff or shortcrust pastry, thawed if frozen

2 eggs, beaten

sea salt and freshly ground black pepper

Mustard Sauce, to serve (see below)

a baking sheet, lightly oiled

serves 8

Put 2 tablespoons of the oil in a frying pan, heat gently, then add the shallots, garlic and mushrooms. Cook for 15 minutes, stirring frequently, until soft but not browned and all the liquid has evaporated. Season with salt and pepper, let cool, then chill in the refrigerator.

Put 1 tablespoon of the oil in a roasting tin and put in a preheated oven at 220°C (425°F) Gas 7 for 5 minutes. Rub the beef fillet all over with the remaining oil and salt and pepper, and transfer to the preheated roasting tin. Cook for 15 minutes, then remove from the oven. Transfer the fillet to a plate, reserving the meat juices for the mustard sauce (below), and let cool until completely cold. (At this stage, you can make the mustard sauce in the roasting tin and reheat it when you need it.)

Roll out the pastry to a rectangle large enough to wrap around the fillet. Brush lightly with the beaten eggs. Spoon the mushroom mixture evenly over the pastry, leaving a 5 cm border all around the edges. Put the cold beef fillet in the middle of the pastry, on top of the mushrooms, and either roll the pastry around the fillet or wrap, as if covering a parcel. Try not to have too much pastry at the ends, and trim to avoid areas of double pastry. Turn the parcel so that the seam is underneath, and transfer to a lightly oiled baking sheet. Brush all over with the beaten eggs and chill for 2 hours.

Cook the beef parcel on the middle shelf of a preheated oven at 200°C (400°F) Gas 6 for 20 minutes. Lower the oven to 180°C (350°F) Gas 4 and continue cooking for 15 minutes for rare, 35 minutes for medium and 50 minutes for well done. If you are cooking to well done, you may need to reduce the oven temperature to prevent the pastry from burning while the beef cooks through. To serve, cut the beef parcel into thick slices and serve with the mustard sauce.

mustard sauce

2 tablespoons smooth Dijon mustard

2 tablespoons wholegrain mustard

100 ml white wine

400 ml double cream

reserved juices from roasting the beef fillet

serves 8

This sauce is rather delicious but also rich, so a little goes a long way.

Put the mustards, white wine, double cream and roasting juices in a saucepan (if not making in the roasting tin, see above). Bring to the boil, then simmer for 5 minutes. If you are making it in advance, after roasting the fillet, make it in the roasting tin. Serve hot with the beef.

FAMILY GATHERINGS

Now that you are married, there will be times when you will want to entertain your family and your in-laws – a great opportunity to show off your new crockery, glasses and tableware. Take the stress out of preparing for these gatherings with this delicious selection of ideas that are bound to impress. There are suggestions for summer and winter get-togethers, as well as some tempting dishes for vegetarian relatives.

roasted vegetable dauphinois

1 garlic clove

butter, for brushing

400 g parsnips, topped, tailed
and cut into 1 cm
diagonal slices

a handful of fresh sage leaves

350 g carrots, cut into
1 cm diagonal slices

350 g uncooked beetroot,
scrubbed well and cut into
1 cm diagonal slices

275 ml double cream

1 tablespoon olive oil

sea salt and freshly ground
black pepper

*a baking dish, about
30 cm square*

serves 4

This rich, creamy, garlicky sauce is offset by the earthy flavours of root vegetables, plus the slightly tart and highly aromatic sage. It is easy to prepare, and non-vegetarians will love it too – it's delicious with lamb. Serve with roasted potatoes and a herby salad with mustard dressing.

Rub the garlic around the base and sides of the baking dish, then brush with butter. Pack overlapping slices of parsnips into the dish. Season well with salt and pepper, then add one-third of the sage leaves.

Repeat the process, first with the carrots, then the beetroot, seasoning each layer with salt and pepper and dotting with the remaining sage. Pour over the cream.

Cover the dish with foil and bake in a preheated oven at 200°C (400°F) Gas 6 for 1 hour 40 minutes. Remove the foil and lightly sprinkle the vegetables with the olive oil. Return to the oven and continue cooking for a further 20 minutes or until the vegetables are very tender.

leek, feta & black olive tart

This tart can be made with a multitude of complementary toppings: onion, thyme and blue cheese; wild mushroom and goats' cheese; or spinach, ricotta and pine nuts.

Roll out the pastry to fit the tin almost exactly. Trim and discard a tiny strip around the edge of the pastry so that it will rise evenly.

Heat a wok or frying pan, add the oil and leeks and stir-fry until beginning to soften. Add just a little salt, then stir in the dill. Transfer to a colander to drain. Let cool.

Arrange the leeks over the pastry, then top with the feta and olives. Bake in a preheated oven at 200°C (400°F) Gas 6 for 35 minutes or until the pastry has risen and is golden brown. Serve with a salad of mixed leaves.

375 g puff pastry,
thawed if frozen

1 tablespoon olive oil

400 g leeks, thinly sliced

a large handful of fresh dill,
coarsely chopped

200 g feta cheese, cut into
small cubes

100 g pitted black olives

sea salt

mixed salad leaves, to serve

a baking tin, about 30 x 20 cm

serves 4-6

This tart is made extra special by blending in a little smoked salmon (you could also use gravadlax) at the same time as the eggs and cream. This gives the tart a mysterious, slightly smoky flavour and a velvety texture.

salmon, dill & parmesan tart
with pickled cucumber

1 recipe Pâte Brisée (see page 182)

salmon and dill filling

450 g fresh salmon fillets (with or without skin)

300 ml double cream

75 g smoked salmon pieces (scraps will do, but cut off any brown bits)

3 eggs, beaten

3 tablespoons chopped fresh dill, plus extra dill sprigs to garnish

25 g freshly grated Parmesan cheese

sea salt and freshly ground black pepper

cucumber topping

2 large cucumbers

1 tablespoon sea salt

1 tablespoon caster sugar

100 ml white wine or cider vinegar

2 tablespoons chopped fresh dill

freshly ground white pepper

a tart tin, 25 cm diameter

foil or baking parchment and baking beans

a baking sheet

serves 6-8

Bring the pastry to room temperature. Roll it out thinly on a lightly floured work surface, then use to line the tart tin. Chill or freeze for 15 minutes. Line the pastry case with foil, baking parchment or all-purpose clingfilm (flicking the edges inwards towards the centre so that they don't catch on the pastry), then fill with baking beans. Set on a baking sheet and bake blind in the centre of a preheated oven at 200°C (400°F) Gas 6 for 10–12 minutes.

Remove the foil, baking parchment or clingfilm and the baking beans and return the pastry case to the oven for a further 5–7 minutes to dry out completely. Remove from the oven and reduce the oven temperature to 190°C (375°F) Gas 5.

Put the salmon fillets in a shallow pan and cover them with cold water. Add a little salt and bring slowly to the boil. Just before the water boils, turn off the heat and leave the salmon in the water until it is cold – by then it will be cooked and moist. Lift it out of the water and drain well. Peel off any skin and check for any bones. Flake coarsely.

Put the cream in a blender, add the smoked salmon and eggs, then blend until smooth. Season well with salt and pepper and stir in the dill. Sprinkle the salmon flakes over the base of the tart and pour in the smoked salmon and cream mixture. Sprinkle with the Parmesan, set on a baking sheet and bake in the preheated oven for 25 minutes, until just set. Remove from the oven and let cool completely.

Meanwhile, to make the cucumber topping, peel the cucumbers, then slice them as thinly as possible using a mandoline or a food processor. Spread in a colander and sprinkle with the salt, mixing well. Stand the colander on a plate and leave to drain for 30 minutes. Rinse well and squeeze the excess moisture out of the cucumbers. Spread the cucumbers over a large plate.

Dissolve the sugar in the vinegar and stir in the dill. Pour this over the cucumber and let marinate for at least 1 hour before serving.

To serve, drain the cucumbers well and arrange them casually over the top of the salmon tart. Grind over lots of white pepper, top with dill sprigs, then serve immediately. Any extra cucumber salad can be served on the side.

Good fishmongers will make sure the thin grey membrane that lies under the skin is removed; but if it isn't, insist that it is, all the way down the tail, because it's a difficult job to do at home.

whole roast monkfish

about 12 thin slices of smoked bacon or pancetta – enough to cover the fish

1 monkfish tail, about 600 g

2 tablespoons extra virgin olive oil

200 g mushrooms, sliced

2 large garlic cloves, crushed

250 ml dry white wine

1 kg tomatoes, skinned (see page 49), deseeded and chopped

2 tablespoons crème fraîche

a handful of fresh basil leaves, chopped

coarse sea salt

serves 4

Set the bacon on a work surface with the slices slightly overlapping each other. Put the monkfish on top, belly up. Wrap it in the bacon with the ends of the bacon overlapping across the belly. Turn the fish over and set aside.

Heat the oil in a large frying pan. Add the mushrooms and a pinch of salt and cook until browned, 3–5 minutes. Stir in the garlic, then add the wine and cook over high heat for 1 minute. Stir in the tomatoes, salt lightly and simmer gently for 5 minutes.

Pour the tomato sauce into a baking dish just large enough to hold the fish. Set the fish on top and roast in a preheated oven at 220°C (425°F) Gas 7 for 15 minutes. Lower the oven to 200°C (400°F) Gas 6 and roast for 30 minutes more. Remove from the oven and transfer the fish to a plate. Stir the crème fraîche and basil into the tomato sauce. Set the monkfish back on top and serve.

hake in green sauce

12 mussels (to clean them, see note on page 59)

16 clams

90 ml cava sparkling wine

4 hake steaks cut through the bone, about 200 g each (leave the bone in)

150 ml olive oil

4 garlic cloves, thinly sliced

1 tablespoon finely chopped fresh flat leaf parsley

1 tablespoon finely chopped fresh coriander

sea salt

serves 4

Put the mussels, clams and wine in a saucepan over high heat. As the shellfish open, remove them to a bowl and cover with clingfilm. Discard any that fail to open. Strain the cooking juices through a muslin-lined sieve and set aside.

Put the hake on a plate and sprinkle with a little salt 10 minutes before cooking.

Put the oil and garlic in a heavy-based frying pan and heat gently so the garlic turns golden slowly and doesn't burn. Remove the garlic with a slotted spoon and set aside until ready to serve.

Pour two-thirds of the oil from the pan into a jug and reserve. Add the hake to the oil left in the pan. Cook over very low heat moving the pan in a circular motion – keep taking it off the heat so it doesn't cook too quickly (the idea is to encourage the oozing of the juices instead of letting them fry and burn). Add the reserved oil bit by bit as you move the pan, so an emulsion starts to form. When all the oil has been added, remove the fish to a plate and keep it warm. Put the pan on the heat, add the reserved clam juices and stir to form the sauce.

Return the fish to the pan, add the chopped parsley and coriander and continue to cook until the fish is done, about 5 minutes. Just before serving, add the opened mussels, clams and fried garlic to the pan to heat through. Serve.

Basting the chicken a few times as it cooks will help to keep it moist. To do so, remove the chicken from the oven every 30 minutes or so and spoon the wine juices over the top. Don't over-baste or you will lower the oven temperature and the estimated cooking time will be altered.

whole roasted chicken
with prunes & thyme

1 chicken, about 1.8 kg
4 red onions, peeled and cut into 6 wedges
250 g ready-to-eat prunes
600 ml red wine
1 teaspoon caster sugar
a bunch of thyme sprigs
25 g butter
sea salt and freshly ground black pepper

kitchen string

serves 4

Loosely tie the legs of the chicken together with string to ensure it keeps its plump shape while cooking. Sprinkle with salt and pepper and put it in a large roasting tin. Put the onions and prunes around the chicken and pour the wine over the top. Sprinkle with the sugar and thyme sprigs, then dot the butter over the chicken.

Roast the chicken in a preheated oven at 200°C (400°F) Gas 6 for about 1½ hours, basting frequently, until the chicken is dark golden brown and cooked all the way through. To test for doneness, use a small knife or skewer to pierce the thickest part of the leg through to the bone – it is cooked when the juices that run out are clear and there is no trace of pink.

Remove the chicken to a board, carve and serve with the onions and prunes.

You can roast potatoes in other oils, such as sunflower, or even in lard, but olive oil is much the healthiest, and delicious with it. The sprinkled flour gives the perfect coating to make the outsides crisp. If you don't have rock salt, which adds an extra crunch, use sea salt instead.

roasted potatoes

1 kg potatoes, peeled and cut into 5 cm pieces
150 ml olive oil
25 g butter
1 tablespoon plain flour, seasoned with
rock salt and freshly ground black pepper

serves 4

Put the potatoes in a large saucepan, cover with cold water, salt lightly, then bring to the boil. Reduce the heat and simmer for 8 minutes to par-boil.

Meanwhile, pour the olive oil into a roasting tin and add the butter. Put in a preheated oven at 220°C (425°F) Gas 7 for 5 minutes, until smoking hot. Drain the potatoes well and return them to the saucepan. Holding the lid on, shake the pan well to roughen the surface of the potatoes.

Add the potatoes to the roasting tin and turn them over with a large metal spoon to coat them all over with oil. Sprinkle with the flour, then roast for 45–50 minutes until crisp and golden. Use a large, metal spoon to push the potatoes around the tin from time to time during cooking, to prevent them from sticking.

This makes the perfect dish to serve for a long Sunday family lunch. Start with apéritifs and nibbles, then serve this with boiled baby new potatoes and a good red wine. Follow with a cheese platter. An apple tart (see page 152) before coffee makes the perfect ending.

spring lamb stew *with vegetables*

Heat the oil in a large casserole, add the lamb and brown the pieces on all sides, in batches if necessary. When all the lamb has been browned, return it all to the pan, lower the heat slightly and stir in a pinch of salt and the flour. Cook, stirring to coat evenly, for 1 minute.

Add the tomatoes and garlic to the pan, then stir in the stock, bay leaf and thyme. Bring to the boil and skim off any foam that rises to the surface. Reduce the heat, then cover and simmer gently for 40 minutes.

Add the carrots, leeks and turnips and cook for 25 minutes more. Taste and adjust the seasoning with salt and pepper.

Add the peas and cook for 7 minutes. Sprinkle with the parsley and serve immediately.

1 tablespoon sunflower oil

700 g lamb neck fillet, cubed

500 g lamb chump chops, each one cut into several pieces

1 tablespoon plain flour

2 ripe tomatoes, skinned (see page 49), deseeded and chopped

2 garlic cloves, crushed

600 ml fresh lamb or chicken stock

1 fresh bay leaf

a sprig of fresh thyme

4 baby carrots, cut into 3 cm pieces

200 g baby leeks, trimmed and cut into 5 cm lengths

200 g baby turnips

200 g sugar snap peas

a handful of fresh flat leaf parsley, chopped

coarse sea salt and freshly ground black pepper

serves 4

4 thick-cut pork chops

extra virgin olive oil

coarse sea salt and freshly ground black pepper

mustard and vinegar sauce

60 ml wine, dry white or red

250 ml fresh chicken stock

60 ml tarragon or sherry vinegar

40 g unsalted butter

3 shallots, finely chopped

1 tablespoon plain flour

2 teaspoons tomato purée

1 teaspoon coarse Dijon mustard

8 French cornichons, sliced

a sprig of fresh tarragon, leaves stripped and chopped

a small handful of fresh flat leaf parsley, chopped

a stove-top grill pan

serves 2–4

pork chops *with piquant sauce*

To make the sauce, put the wine and stock in a small saucepan. Bring to the boil for 1 minute, then stir in the vinegar. Set aside.

Melt the butter in another saucepan. Add the shallots and cook until soft, 3–5 minutes. Add the flour and cook, stirring for 1 minute. Add the warm stock mixture and tomato purée and mix well. Simmer gently for 15 minutes.

Meanwhile, remove the rind from the pork chops. Rub a ridged stove-top grill pan with the oil and heat on high. When hot, add the pork chops and cook for 4–5 minutes. Turn and cook the other side for 3–4 minutes. Remove from the heat and season the chops on both sides with salt and pepper.

Stir the mustard, cornichons, tarragon and parsley into the sauce and serve immediately, with the pork chops.

Only the very best meat should be used for this delicious roast, and you are in the hands of your butcher for that, so choose him well! The art is not so much in the cooking as in the timing, so you don't end up with everybody waiting for you at the table, while you have forgotten to make the gravy or put the Yorkshire pudding in early enough. This timetable, for serving a roast at 1:00 pm, assumes 3 kg beef on the bone, which will take about 1 hour 40 minutes plus 20 minutes resting time – 2 hours in all.

roast beef *with all the trimmings*

3 kg bone-in forerib of beef (2–3 bones)

2 tablespoons plain flour

1 tablespoon English mustard powder

75 g beef dripping, shortening or 4 tablespoons olive oil

3 onions, quartered

8–10 potatoes, cut into chunks and par-boiled (see page 103)

5–6 parsnips, halved lengthways

sea salt and freshly ground black pepper

accompaniments

1 recipe Horseradish Sauce (see page 181)

1 recipe Yorkshire Pudding (see page 185)

1.25 kg green vegetable, such as cabbage, sliced and steamed or boiled

1 recipe Gravy (see page 178)

an instant-read thermometer

serves 8-10

10:45	Preheat the oven to 240°C (475°F) Gas 8. Season the meat with salt and pepper, mix the flour and the mustard powder and pat it onto the beef fat. Put the dripping or oil in the roasting tin, put the onions in the middle and set the beef, fat side up, on top.
11:00	Put the potatoes and parsnips around the meat and put the tin in the oven.
11:10	Make the horseradish sauce as directed on page 181 and set aside.
11:20	Reduce oven temperature to 190°C (375°F) Gas 5, baste the beef and turn the vegetables in the fat.
11:40	Baste the beef and turn the potatoes and parsnips in the fat.
12:10	Repeat.
12:29	Increase the oven temperature to 240°C (475°F) Gas 8 and spoon 4 tablespoons of the fat into the large Yorkshire pudding tin, if using.
12:30	Heat the fat on the top of the stove and pour the Yorkshire pudding batter into the tin, or wait to do this until 12:42 if you are making individual ones (see below).
12:31	Put the Yorkshire pudding tin in the oven.
12:33	Put the green vegetable on to boil. Insert a meat thermometer into the beef.
12:40	Take the beef out now, or when the thermometer registers 60°C (175°F) (or a little below if you like beef very rare). Lift the beef onto a serving dish, then the vegetables and set aside in a warm place. It will go on cooking as it rests.
12:42	Spoon off the fat and retain it for another time, or spoon into the small Yorkshire pudding tins, pour in the batter, then put in the oven.
12:45	Make the gravy in the roasting tin and pour into a gravy boat.
12:50	Dish up the green vegetable and keep it warm.
12:58	Serve the Yorkshire pudding around the beef or on a separate platter.
1:00	Put the beef on the table with the horseradish sauce and the gravy.

butternut squash
with pistou

Butternut and pistou aren't obvious partners, but the sweetness of squash goes very well with the garlicky basil sauce. This is best served with roast lamb or chicken because the pistou makes a lovely sauce for it all.

6 tablespoons extra virgin olive oil

4 garlic cloves

a large handful of fresh basil leaves

2 butternut squash, about 800 g each, trimmed

fine sea salt

serves 4

To make the pistou, put the oil, garlic, basil leaves and a pinch of salt in a small food processor. Blend well. Transfer to a small bowl. Alternatively, to prepare without a machine, crush the garlic, chop the basil leaves, then mix with the oil and salt.

Cut the squash in half lengthways and scoop out the seeds. Arrange the squash halves in a roasting tin and sprinkle with salt. Brush generously with the pistou, letting it well up a bit in the cavity if you like. Roast in a preheated oven at 200°C (400°F) Gas 6 until just browned at the edges and tender when pierced with a knife, 40–45 minutes. Serve hot, with the remaining pistou.

Which vegetables are good for roasting?

- *All root vegetables are good roasted, such as potatoes, carrots, parsnips, sweet potatoes and beetroot.*
- *Most of the onion family – including onions (whole, halved or in wedges), shallots and garlic.*
- *Starchy vegetables like pumpkin and butternut squash.*
- *Squashy ones like peppers, courgettes and aubergines.*

---

savoy cabbage
with bacon & cream

Based loosely on a traditional French dish that includes pheasant, this recipe is a very elegant way to dress up a rustic vegetable. It goes best with poultry and potatoes, both roasted.

1 bay leaf

1 Savoy cabbage, about 1.25 kg

2 tablespoons unsalted butter

1 tablespoon extra virgin olive oil

100 g thinly sliced pancetta, chopped

a sprig of fresh sage, leaves stripped and thinly sliced

4 tablespoons crème fraîche or double cream

sea salt and freshly ground black pepper

serves 4

Bring a large saucepan of water to the boil with the bay leaf and a large pinch of salt. Quarter the cabbage and blanch in the boiling water for 2–3 minutes. Drain well.

Core the cabbage quarters, then slice crossways.

Heat the butter and oil in a large frying pan. Add the pancetta and sage and cook over high heat, stirring often, for 1 minute. Add the cabbage and a pinch of salt and cook, stirring often, for 2–3 minutes.

Stir in the cream and cook until warmed through, about 1 minute. Season generously with pepper and mix well. Add salt to taste and serve hot.

Here, thyme and crème fraîche transform ordinary
boiled carrots into something sumptuous.

carrots *with cream & herbs*

800 g mini carrots, trimmed,
or medium carrots

50 g unsalted butter

a sprig of thyme

2 tablespoons crème fraîche

several sprigs of chervil

a small bunch of chives

fine sea salt

serves 4

If using larger carrots, cut them diagonally into 5 cm slices. Put in a large saucepan (the carrots should fit in almost a single layer for even cooking). Add the butter and set over low heat. Cook to melt the butter and coat, about 3 minutes. Half fill the saucepan with water, then add a pinch of salt and the thyme. Cover and cook until the water is almost completely evaporated, 10–20 minutes.

Stir in the crème fraîche and add salt to taste. Using kitchen scissors, snip the chervil and chives over the top, mix well and serve.

Variation In spring, when turnips are sweet, they make a nice addition to this dish. Peel and quarter large turnips, or just peel baby ones – the main thing is to ensure that all the vegetable pieces (carrot and turnip) are about the same size so that they cook evenly. Halve the carrot quantity and complete with turnips, or double the recipe. Sprinkle with a large handful of just-cooked shelled peas before serving for extra crunch and pretty colour.

French beans are the classic accompaniment for lamb,
but they are equally delicious with fish and chicken.

french beans *with garlic*

Bring a large saucepan of water to the boil. Add the beans and cook for 3–4 minutes from the time the water returns to the boil. Drain and refresh under cold running water. Set aside.

Heat the oil and butter in a frying pan. Add the garlic, beans and salt, and cook over high heat for 1 minute, stirring. Remove from the heat and stir in the parsley and lemon juice, if using. Sprinkle with pepper and serve.

Variation For mixed beans, halve the quantity of green beans and add a 400 g jar of drained French flageolet beans to the cooked green beans when frying with the garlic. Instead of lemon juice, stir in 3–4 tablespoons crème fraîche just before serving.

625 g small green beans

2 tablespoons extra virgin olive oil

1 tablespoon unsalted butter

2 garlic cloves, crushed

a handful of fresh flat leaf parsley, chopped

1 teaspoon freshly squeezed lemon juice (optional)

coarse sea salt and freshly ground black pepper

serves 4

EASY ENTERTAINING

*One of the greatest joys of cooking is entertaining
friends. There is something very satisfying about getting
a group of people around your table and preparing good
food for everyone to share. When you invite friends to
dinner, you won't want to spend all evening in the
kitchen, missing out on the fun. So these recipes are
quick to prepare, or can be prepared ahead of time,
so you, too, can enjoy the company as much as the food.*

onion tart

Every good cook should be able to make a savoury tart, and this has to be one of the most popular and delicious. As it bakes, it fills your home with gorgeous baking aromas – your guests will be impressed.

250 g plain flour

175 g chilled butter, cut into small pieces

2 eggs, beaten

Tomato Salsa, to serve (see below)

filling

75 g butter

2 tablespoons olive oil

500 g onions, thinly sliced

2 eggs

125 ml single cream

sea salt and freshly ground black pepper

a tart tin, 20 cm diameter

baking parchment and baking beans or uncooked rice

serves 4

Sift the flour into a large bowl and add the butter. Using your fingertips, rub the butter into the flour until the mixture looks like fine breadcrumbs. Add the beaten eggs and, using a round-bladed knife, cut through the mixture until it forms a ball. Knead lightly in the bowl with floured hands until evenly mixed, then cover and chill in the refrigerator for 20 minutes.

Roll out the pastry on a lightly floured work surface to a circle at least 5 cm bigger in diameter than the base of the tart tin. Drape the pastry over the rolling pin, carefully lift it up and lay it over the top of the tin. Gently press the pastry into the tin, making sure there are no air pockets, then use a sharp knife to trim off the excess pastry. Chill the pastry case in the refrigerator for 20 minutes.

To make the filling, heat the butter and oil in a saucepan, add the onions and cook over low heat for 30 minutes until soft and translucent, but not brown.

Line the pastry with baking parchment and baking beans or rice and bake in a preheated oven at 200°C (400°F) Gas 6 for 20 minutes. Remove the baking beans or rice and parchment, reduce to 160°C (325°F) Gas 3 and cook for a further 15 minutes until the pastry is set and lightly golden.

Put the eggs and cream in a large bowl and beat until mixed. Add the onions with salt and pepper to taste. Pour into the pastry case and bake in the oven for 25 minutes until set and golden. Serve warm or cold with tomato salsa.

tomato salsa

4 tomatoes, skinned (see page 49)

3 spring onions, chopped

freshly squeezed juice of 1 lemon

a bunch of fresh flat leaf parsley, chopped

sea salt and freshly ground black pepper

serves 4

Cut each tomato into quarters, remove and discard the core and seeds, then chop the flesh. Put in a bowl and add the spring onions, lemon juice, parsley and salt and pepper, to taste. Mix well, then set aside for 2 hours to let the flavours develop. Serve with the onion tart.

A comforting bowl of risotto is always a welcome treat for guests, and this version is particularly creamy and satisfying. Gorgonzola is a strong Italian cheese with blue-green marbling that works well alongside the cool ricotta in this recipe.

gorgonzola & ricotta risotto
with crisp sage leaves

about 1.5 litres hot chicken stock or Vegetable Stock (see page 178)

125 g unsalted butter

1 onion, finely chopped

400 g risotto rice

75 ml dry white vermouth

1 tablespoon chopped fresh sage leaves

75 g Gorgonzola cheese, crumbled

75 g fresh ricotta cheese

sea salt and freshly ground black pepper

crisp sage leaves

about 30 fresh sage leaves with stalks

oil, for deep-frying

an electric deep-fryer or wok

serves 4

To make the crisp sage leaves, pat them thoroughly dry with kitchen paper. Heat the oil to 180°C (350°F) in a deep-fryer or wok. If using a deep-fryer, put the leaves in the basket and lower into the oil. It will hiss alarmingly, but don't worry. Immediately the hissing has stopped, lift the basket out and shake off the excess oil. (If using a wok, use tongs or a slotted spoon to remove the leaves.) Put the leaves on kitchen paper to drain. Season with a sprinkling of salt and set aside. They will crisp up as they cool.

Put the stock in a saucepan and keep at a gentle simmer. Melt half the butter in a large, heavy saucepan and add the onion. Cook gently for 10 minutes until soft, golden and translucent but not browned. Add the rice and stir until well coated with the butter and heated through. Pour in the vermouth and boil hard until reduced and almost disappeared. This will remove the taste of raw alcohol. Stir in the chopped fresh sage leaves.

Begin adding the stock, a large ladle at a time, stirring gently until each ladle has been almost absorbed by the rice. The risotto should be kept at a bare simmer throughout cooking, so don't let the rice dry out – add more stock as necessary. About halfway through the cooking time, stir in the Gorgonzola until melted. Continue adding stock and cooking until the rice is tender and creamy, but the grains still firm. (This should take 15–20 minutes depending on the type of rice used – check the packet instructions.) The risotto should be quite loose, but not soupy.

Taste and season well with salt and pepper and beat in the ricotta and remaining butter. Cover and let rest for a couple of minutes so the risotto can relax. You may like to add a little more hot stock to the risotto just before you serve to loosen it, but don't let it wait around too long or the rice will turn mushy. Serve with the fried sage leaves sprinkled on top.

Spaghettini with clams is typically Italian. Shellfish make a quick
pasta dish special – perfect for entertaining.

baby clam sauce

500 g spaghettini, freshly cooked

vongole sauce

1 kg small fresh clams, in their shells

125–150 ml olive oil

1 garlic clove, peeled but left whole

a piece of dried chilli

2 handfuls of fresh parsley,
finely chopped

to serve

freshly ground black pepper

chopped fresh parsley

extra virgin olive oil

serves 4-6

Wash the clams in plenty of running water until not a trace of sand is left. Drain well. Put them in a heavy-based saucepan over high heat. Cover with a lid and shake the pan until all the clams have opened (remove and discard any that do not open). Strain off the liquid, pour it through a fine sieve and reserve.

Heat the olive oil in a large saucepan, add the garlic and chilli and heat through gently. When the garlic starts to turn golden, discard it and the chilli. Add the clams to the pan, together with their strained cooking liquid. Add the parsley and cook gently for 1–2 minutes for the flavours to blend.

Add the clams and their sauce to the freshly cooked spaghettini and mix well. Tip onto a large serving plate and top with lots of black pepper, some more parsley and olive oil. Serve at once.

Variation To make a tomato version of this sauce, skin, deseed and chop 500 g plum tomatoes. Add them to the oil at the same time as the garlic and chilli. Cook over low heat for 20–30 minutes until reduced to a creamy mass. Add the clams and the strained juices and cook for 1–2 minutes for the flavours to blend. Add the parsley and proceed as in the main recipe.

24 large uncooked prawns,
shelled and deveined

4 tablespoons Chilli Oil (see page 181)

freshly squeezed juice of 1 lemon

sea salt and freshly ground black pepper

pistachio and mint pesto

50 g shelled pistachio nuts

a bunch of mint leaves

1 garlic clove, crushed

2 spring onions, chopped

125 ml extra virgin olive oil

1 tablespoon white wine vinegar

to serve

1 lemon, cut into wedges

crusty bread

serves 4

prawns *with chilli oil & pistachio & mint pesto*

To make the pesto, put the nuts, mint, garlic and spring onions in a food processor and blend coarsely. Add the oil and blend until fairly smooth and bright green. Stir in the vinegar and season to taste with salt and pepper. Set aside while you prepare the prawns, or store in a screw-top jar in the refrigerator for up to 5 days.

Put the prawns in a shallow dish and sprinkle with the chilli oil, salt and pepper. Cover and let marinate for at least 30 minutes or longer, if possible.

When ready to serve, thread the prawns onto skewers and cook on a preheated barbecue or under a hot grill for about 2 minutes on each side until charred and tender – the flesh should be just opaque. Do not overcook the prawns or they will be tough.

Transfer to separate plates or a large platter. Sprinkle with the lemon juice and serve with the pesto, lemon wedges and crusty bread to mop up the juices.

seared swordfish
with avocado & salsa

Put the oil, lime zest and juice in a small bowl and whisk well. Add plenty of black pepper. Put the swordfish steaks in a shallow dish and pour over the oil and lime mixture, making sure the fish is coated on both sides. Cover and refrigerate for up to 1 hour.

Meanwhile, to make the salsa, put the onion, chilli, tomato, oil, lime zest and juice in a bowl. Mix gently, then cover and refrigerate.

Preheat a stove-top grill pan or barbecue until hot and cook the fish for 2–3 minutes on each side or until just cooked through. Transfer the swordfish to 4 serving plates. Divide the avocado slices between the 4 plates, spoon over the salsa, sprinkle with coriander and serve with lime wedges.

2 tablespoons olive oil

grated zest and juice of 2 unwaxed limes

4 swordfish steaks

2 large, just-ripe avocados, halved, pitted, peeled and sliced

freshly ground black pepper

salsa

1 small red onion, chopped

1 red chilli, deseeded and very finely chopped

1 large ripe tomato, halved, deseeded and chopped

3 tablespoons extra virgin olive oil

grated zest and juice of 1 unwaxed lime

to serve

a bunch of coriander, chopped

1 lime, cut into wedges

a stove-top grill pan (optional)

serves 4

peppered tuna steak *with salsa rossa*

Salsa rossa is one of those divine Italian sauces that transforms simple meat and fish dishes into food nirvana. The slight sweetness from the red pepper is a good foil for the spicy pepper crust.

To make the salsa rossa, grill the pepper until charred all over, then put it in a plastic bag and let cool. Peel and discard the skin, then remove the seeds, reserving any juices. Chop the flesh.

Heat the oil gently in a frying pan, then add the garlic and sauté for 3 minutes. Add the tomatoes, chilli flakes and oregano and simmer gently for 15 minutes. Stir in the chopped pepper and the vinegar and simmer for a further 5 minutes to evaporate any excess liquid. Transfer to a blender and purée until fairly smooth. Add salt and pepper to taste and let cool. It may be stored in a screw-top jar in the refrigerator for up to 3 days.

Put the crushed peppercorns on a large plate. Brush the tuna steaks with oil, then press the crushed peppercorns into both sides of the tuna. Preheat a stove-top grill pan or barbecue until hot, add the tuna and cook for 1 minute on each side. Wrap the tuna loosely in foil and let rest for 5 minutes before serving with the salsa rossa and mixed salad leaves.

6 tablespoons mixed peppercorns, coarsely crushed

6 tuna steaks, 200 g each

1 tablespoon extra virgin olive oil

mixed salad leaves, to serve

salsa rossa

1 large red pepper

1 tablespoon extra virgin olive oil

2 garlic cloves, crushed

2 large ripe tomatoes, peeled (see page 49) and roughly chopped

a small pinch of dried chilli flakes

1 tablespoon dried oregano

1 tablespoon red wine vinegar

sea salt and freshly ground black pepper

a stove-top grill pan (optional)

serves 6

Baked chicken, swimming in this lemony, spicy marinade, makes easy entertaining. Thighs are the best choice, because they stay tender and moist, though you could use a whole chicken cut into pieces.

lemon-spiced chicken

12–16 chicken pieces, preferably thighs (allow 3–4 per person)

5 tablespoons extra virgin olive oil

freshly squeezed juice of 2 lemons

1 tablespoon ground cumin

1 teaspoon sweet smoked paprika

½ teaspoon chilli flakes

1 teaspoon dried oregano

a small bunch of thyme sprigs, fresh or dried

2 teaspoons coarse sea salt

1 teaspoon coarsely ground black pepper

Bulghur Wheat Pilaf, to serve (see below), optional

a baking dish

serves 4

Trim any excess fat from the chicken pieces. Put the chicken in a baking dish large enough to hold them comfortably (or divide between 2 dishes). Put the oil, lemon juice, cumin, paprika, chilli flakes, oregano, thyme, salt and pepper in a bowl and mix well. Pour over the chicken and turn to coat well. Cover and set aside for at least 30 minutes, or refrigerate for 6–8 hours.

Make sure all the chicken pieces are skin side up in the dish and roast in a preheated oven at 200°C (400°F) Gas 6 until browned and cooked through, 50–60 minutes. Serve straight away with the pan juices poured over, and accompanied by the bulghur wheat pilaf, if liked.

This is intended as an accompaniment, but if you add some bacon, chopped peppers, mushrooms, cooked peas, wilted spinach or crumbled feta, you could serve it as a light meal.

bulghur wheat pilaf

2 tablespoons extra virgin olive oil

a handful of vermicelli or cappellini, about 35 g

250 g bulghur wheat

600 ml unsalted fresh chicken or Vegetable Stock (see page 178)

a few sprigs of thyme

sea salt

serves 4

Heat the oil in a saucepan, break the vermicelli or cappellini into small pieces as you add them to the pan and cook, stirring regularly, until browned, about 5 minutes. Stir in the bulghur and a good pinch of salt and mix to coat the grains.

Add the stock and thyme, stir and bring to the boil. Cover, lower the heat and cook, undisturbed, until all the liquid has been absorbed, 10–15 minutes.

Fluff up the grains with a fork and serve hot.

Braising is a fantastic way to cook thick pork chops, because it makes the meat so tender. Chicken pieces would work equally well. The flavours in this dish point straight to Spain, though it is not traditional. This recipe cries out for advance preparation – the orange, chilli and everything else need time to mingle and develop the flavours – which makes it ideal for entertaining. It's very homely sort of food and perfect with potatoes, preferably fried or mashed. Serve it with a good bottle of Rioja wine.

braised pork chops
with tomato, orange & chilli

3 tablespoons extra virgin olive oil

8 bone-in pork chops, about 280 g each, trimmed of fat

3 celery sticks, chopped

1 onion, chopped

4 garlic cloves, finely chopped

½–1 teaspoon chilli flakes

125 ml red wine, preferably Rioja

400 g canned chopped tomatoes

freshly squeezed juice of 1 orange, orange shell reserved

1 bay leaf

a few sprigs of fresh oregano or thyme

a handful of fresh flat leaf parsley, coarsely chopped

sea salt

to serve

Classic Creamy Mashed Potatoes (see page 88)

sugar snap peas, steamed

serves 8

Heat 2 tablespoons of the oil in a large sauté pan with a lid. Add the pork chops and cook until browned, 3–5 minutes. Turn and cook the other side (work in batches if they don't all fit in the pan). Transfer to a plate, season with salt and set aside.

Add the celery and onion to the pan and cook over high heat until browned, 2–3 minutes. Add the garlic and chilli flakes and cook for 30 seconds more. Add the wine and stir, scraping any bits that stick to the bottom of the pan. Boil for 1 minute, then stir in the tomatoes, orange juice, bay leaf, oregano or thyme and salt, to taste. Quarter the orange used for the juice and put 1 piece in the sauce.

Return the meat to the pan and bury it under the sauce as much as possible. Cover, lower the heat and simmer gently until tender, about 1 hour. Turn the meat halfway through cooking.

Remove the meat from the sauce, put it on a heatproof plate and keep warm in a low oven. Raise the heat under the tomato sauce and cook for 3–5 minutes to thicken it slightly. Remove and discard the orange piece, bay leaf and herb sprigs. Pile the sauce on top of the pork chops, sprinkle with chopped parsley and serve with mashed potatoes and steamed sugar snap peas.

The best stews are those that are marinated for 24 hours, then cooked slowly for a long time. Unfortunately, they require a lot of advance planning. That is where this recipe comes in handy; it's a sort of cross between beef stew and ragù sauce, without the forward thinking.

beef provençal

1 bay leaf

a few sprigs of thyme

1 small inner celery stick, with the leaves

2 tablespoons extra virgin olive oil

1 large onion, chopped

1 kg braising beef, such as chuck, cut into 3.5 cm cubes

1 piece of cured ham, preferably a fatty end piece, about 150–200 g

6 garlic cloves, sliced

250 ml dry white or red wine

400 g canned chopped tomatoes

35 g pitted black olives

a handful of fresh basil leaves, chopped

sea salt

1 kg pasta, freshly cooked, to serve

kitchen string

serves 4

Tie the bay leaf, thyme and celery stick together with kitchen string.

Heat the oil in a large frying pan. Add the onion and cook until softened, 2–3 minutes. Add the beef, ham and garlic and cook for 1–2 minutes. Season with salt.

Add the wine, boil for 1 minute, then add the tomatoes and the tied bunch of herbs. Cover, lower the heat and simmer gently until the meat is very tender, about 2 hours.

To serve, remove the bunch of herbs and stir in the olives. The ham can either be removed, shredded and added back to the stew, or simply removed; taste the ham to see which you prefer – sometimes the heel of a cured ham can be quite strong in flavour. Sprinkle with basil leaves and serve over freshly cooked pasta.

4 fillet steaks, about 200 g each

2 tablespoons extra virgin olive oil

sea salt and freshly ground black pepper

horseradish and chive butter

125 g unsalted butter, softened

1½ tablespoons grated fresh horseradish

1 tablespoon chopped fresh chives

to serve (optional)

sautéed potatoes

green salad

serves 4

pan-fried fillet steak
with horseradish & chive butter

To make the horseradish and chive butter, put the butter, horseradish and chives in a bowl and beat well. Season to taste with salt and pepper. Form into a log shape, wrap in foil and chill in the refrigerator for about 30 minutes.

Season the steaks with salt and pepper. Heat the oil in a frying pan and fry the steaks over medium-high heat for 3 minutes on each side for rare, a couple of minutes longer for medium.

Top each steak with 1–2 slices of the horseradish butter and set aside to rest in a warm oven for 5 minutes. Serve with sautéed potatoes and a green salad, if liked.

PUDDINGS

Whether it's something sweet to make a mid-week dinner special or something decadent to round off a family gathering, you will find lots of inspiration here. From fruity puddings for summer such as Apricot and Orange Gelato (see page 143) to warming winter ideas such as Rice Pudding (see page 151), there is something here for every season and every occasion.

apricot & orange gelato

250 g dried apricots, chopped

175 g caster sugar

2 teaspoons freshly grated orange zest and 250 ml freshly squeezed orange juice, about 2–3 unwaxed oranges

3 tablespoons freshly squeezed lemon juice, about 1 medium lemon

1 teaspoon orange flower water

2 tablespoon Cointreau (or other citrus liqueur)

250 g mascarpone cheese, in pieces

400 ml single cream

8–12 wafers, biscuits or sliced brioche, to serve (optional)

an electric ice cream maker or a 1.5 litre freezerproof container with a lid

serves 4-6

Put the chopped apricots in a saucepan and cover with boiling water by about 3 cm. Return to the boil, reduce the heat and simmer for 10 minutes. Remove from the heat and let stand for 5 minutes.

Put the apricots and their cooking water in a blender (for smooth texture) or food processor (for coarse texture), then add the sugar, orange zest and juice, lemon juice, orange flower water and liqueur. Blend well. Add the mascarpone pieces and blend briefly until the mixture is smooth. Pour out half into a large bowl and set aside.

Add the cream to the machine and blend very briefly until incorporated. Pour this into the bowl with the other mixture and stir well. Let cool, if necessary, over iced water.

Transfer the mixture to an ice cream maker and churn for 20–35 minutes or until thick. Spoon into a freezerproof container, cover and freeze until time to use. Alternatively, freeze the mixture in the container, covered, for 6 hours, beating it once, after 3 hours. Serve in scoops or slices with wafers, biscuits or brioche, if using.

Note When sharply flavoured fresh apricots are in season, halve, pit and grill or bake 500 g (8–12 fruit) until they are collapsed, golden and tender. Use these in place of the dried apricots: they need no further cooking.

bitter chocolate & hazelnut gelato

75 g blanched (skinned) hazelnuts, finely chopped

175 g vanilla sugar or caster sugar

150 ml full-fat milk

250 g dark chocolate (at least 70 per cent cocoa solids), broken into pieces

1 tablespoon glucose syrup or corn syrup

1 tablespoon chocolate or hazelnut liqueur or dark rum

400 ml double cream

crisp wafers or biscuits, to serve (optional)

an electric ice cream maker or a 1 litre freezerproof container with a lid

serves 4-6

Put the chopped hazelnuts in a dry frying pan and dry-fry over moderate heat, stirring constantly, until they darken and smell toasty, 2–3 minutes (take care, because they burn easily). Transfer to a plate and let cool.

Put the toasted hazelnuts and 4 tablespoons of the sugar in a small electric spice grinder or coffee grinder. Grind in brief bursts, to a smooth, speckly powder.

Put the milk, chocolate and remaining sugar in a saucepan over very gentle heat. Cook, stirring constantly, until the chocolate melts, then add the glucose syrup and ground sugar and nuts. Remove from the heat, put the pan in a bowl of iced water and let cool. Stir in the liqueur and cream and cool again.

Pour the prepared mixture into an ice cream maker and churn for 20–25 minutes or until set. Alternatively, freeze the mixture in the container, covered, for 6 hours, beating it once, after 3 hours. Serve in scoops with wafers or biscuits, if using.

This amazingly popular pudding actually benefits from being made the day before. For added texture, grind real chocolate in a blender to use for layering and sprinkling.

tiramisù

150 g plain dark chocolate (over 60 per cent cocoa solids)

300 ml double cream

100 ml Italian espresso coffee

6 tablespoons Marsala wine

250 g mascarpone cheese

5 tablespoons caster sugar

2 tablespoons dark rum

2 free-range egg yolks

24 savoiardi

200 g fresh raspberries, plus extra to serve

a serving dish or 4 glasses

serves 4 generously

Put the chocolate in a blender or food processor and grind to a powder. Set aside. Pour the cream into a bowl and whisk until soft peaks form. Set aside.

Pour the espresso into a second bowl and stir in 2 tablespoons of the Marsala. Set aside. Put the mascarpone in a third bowl and whisk in 3 tablespoons of the sugar, then beat in 2 tablespoons of the Marsala and the rum. Set aside.

To make the zabaglione mixture, put the egg yolks, 2 tablespoons Marsala and the remaining 2 tablespoons sugar in a medium heatproof bowl and beat with a hand-held electric mixer or whisk until well blended. Set over a saucepan of gently simmering water – the bottom of the bowl should at no time be in contact with the water, and do not let the water boil. Whisk the mixture until it is glossy, pale, light and fluffy and holds a trail when dropped from the whisk. This should take about 5 minutes. Remove from the heat and whisk until cold. Fold in the whipped cream, then fold in the mascarpone mixture.

Dip the savoiardi, one at a time, into the espresso mixture. Do not leave them in for too long or they will disintegrate. Start assembling the tiramisù by arranging half the dipped savoiardi in the bottom of a serving dish or 4 glasses. Trickle over some of the leftover espresso. Add a layer of raspberries.

Sprinkle with one-third of the ground chocolate, then add half the zabaglione-cream-mascarpone mixture. Arrange the remaining dipped savoiardi on top, moisten with any remaining espresso, add some more raspberries and sprinkle with half the remaining chocolate. Finally spoon over the remaining zabaglione-cream-mascarpone and finish with a thick layer of chocolate and extra raspberries. Chill in the refrigerator for at least 3 hours (overnight is better) to let the flavours develop. Serve chilled.

raspberries in champagne jelly

Put 3 tablespoons hot water in a small heatproof bowl and sprinkle in the gelatine. Set aside in a warm place to dissolve, about 10 minutes. Divide the raspberries between the glasses. Open the champagne and add a little to the dissolved gelatine. Transfer the mixture to a large jug and add the remaining champagne. Mix gently so that you don't build up a froth. Pour this over the raspberries and chill until set, about 2 hours.

25 g powdered gelatine

500 g raspberries

1 bottle champagne, at room temperature

8 glasses

serves 8

Pure indulgence is a crisp meringue with a soft, marshmallow centre, filled with whipped cream and topped with berries. Once mastered, you'll discover that a meringue is one of the simplest, prettiest and most versatile of all puddings. Sharp-flavoured fruits, such as raspberries, balance the sweetness of the meringue, though you could use any of your favourite fruits.

raspberry roulade

6 egg whites, at room temperature (see box, below)

a pinch of sea salt

375 g caster sugar

2 teaspoons cornflour

1 teaspoon white wine vinegar

raspberry rose filling
500 ml double cream

3–6 tablespoons rose water

250 g raspberries

a 30 x 40 cm shallow cake tin, lined with baking parchment

serves 8–10

Put the egg whites and salt in a scrupulously clean, grease-free bowl and, using an electric hand-held mixer, whisk until stiff peaks form. (Take care: if there is any trace of egg yolk or grease in the bowl, the whites won't whisk properly.)

Sprinkle in 1 tablespoon of sugar at a time and whisk between each addition until the meringue is thick and glossy. Add the cornflour and vinegar and whisk until mixed.

Transfer the meringue to the prepared baking tin and, using a spatula, spread it into the corners of the tin and smooth the surface. Bake in a preheated oven at 180°C (350°F) Gas 4 for 17 minutes or until barely crisp. Let cool.

To turn out the meringue, cover with a sheet of baking parchment, then quickly but carefully invert the tin onto the work surface. Lift off the tin, then gently peel off the parchment from the meringue.

To make the filling, put the cream and rose water in a bowl and whisk lightly until soft peaks form. Spoon the cream onto the meringue and spread evenly, leaving a 1 cm border clear all around the edge. Spread the raspberries over the top of the cream.

Lift up the side of the baking parchment nearest to you and use it to help roll up the roulade lengthways. Peel back the paper as you go. Before you reach the end, carefully lift the roulade (still on the parchment) onto a platter or board.

Roll the roulade off the parchment so that the join is underneath. Slice it into 8–10 pieces and serve.

Separating eggs

- *Have 2 bowls ready. Tap the egg on the side of one bowl to crack it in the middle. Using your thumbs, pull open the two halves with the cracked side facing upwards, tipping the yolk into one half and letting any white fall into the bowl. Tip the yolk back and forth between the 2 shell halves until there is no white left around the yolk. Tip the yolk into the other bowl. If any yolk slips into the white, use a shell to scoop it out.*

ricotta cake

5 tablespoons plump raisins

4 tablespoons Cognac

250 g ricotta cheese

250 g mascarpone cheese

4 eggs, separated (see page 147)

4 tablespoons plain flour

grated zest of 1 unwaxed lemon

½ teaspoon ground cinnamon

a pinch of salt

200 g caster sugar

a non-stick cake tin, 22 cm diameter, greased with butter and dusted with flour

serves 4-6

Put the raisins in a small bowl, add the Cognac and let soak for 15–30 minutes.

Put the ricotta, mascarpone and egg yolks in a mixing bowl and beat until well blended. Add the flour, lemon zest, cinnamon, salt and all but about 1 tablespoon of the sugar. Mix well, then set aside.

Put the egg whites and the remaining sugar in another mixing bowl. Beat with an electric hand-held mixer on high until stiff peaks form. Transfer one-third of the egg whites to the ricotta mixture and stir to blend. Using a spatula, gently fold in the remaining egg whites, raisins and Cognac, until no lumps are visible. Pour into the prepared cake tin.

Bake in a preheated oven at 180°C (350°F) Gas 4 until browned around the edges and firm, but still jiggly in the middle, 40–50 minutes. Let cool completely, then cut into wedges and serve at room temperature.

traditional new york cheesecake

200 g digestive biscuits

100 g unsalted butter

75 g caster sugar

filling

150 g unsalted butter

170 g caster sugar

4 large eggs, beaten

30 g plain flour

finely grated zest and juice of 1 large unwaxed lemon

½ teaspoon vanilla essence

675 g full-fat soft cheese, at room temperature

60 ml milk

topping

425 ml sour cream

1 tablespoon icing sugar

freshly squeezed juice of 1 lemon

a springform cake tin, 23 cm diameter, greased

a baking sheet

serves 10-12

To make the crumb base, put the biscuits in a large plastic bag and finely crush them with a rolling pin. Melt the butter in a small saucepan over gentle heat, then stir in the biscuit crumbs and sugar. Spread the mixture over the base of the prepared cake tin, pressing down lightly. Stand the tin on a baking sheet and cook in a preheated oven at 190°C (375°F) Gas 5 for 8–10 minutes. Remove from the oven and let cool. Reduce the oven temperature to 160°C (325°F) Gas 3.

To make the filling, put the butter and sugar in a large bowl and, using a wooden spoon or hand-held electric mixer, beat until pale and fluffy. Gradually beat in the eggs. Mix in the flour, lemon zest and juice and vanilla. Put the soft cheese in a separate bowl and, using a wooden spoon or hand-held electric mixer, beat until smooth. Gently beat in the milk, then gradually beat in the butter and sugar mixture. Spoon the mixture over the crumb base and level the surface. Bake in the preheated oven for 1½ hours.

Meanwhile, to make the topping, put the sour cream, icing sugar and lemon juice in a large bowl and, using a wooden spoon or electric hand mixer, beat lightly. Cover and chill in the refrigerator until required.

Remove the cheesecake from the oven and increase the oven temperature to 190°C (375°F) Gas 5. Pour the topping over the surface of the cheesecake, level with a spatula and return to the oven for a further 10 minutes or until set. Turn off the oven, leave the door ajar and let the cheesecake cool in the oven to prevent it from cracking. Once cool, chill the cheesecake in the refrigerator for 2 hours before serving.

6 peaches, not too ripe

1 tablespoon plain flour

1 tablespoon freshly squeezed lemon juice

3 tablespoons clear honey

cream or vanilla ice cream, to serve

cobbler topping

125 ml double cream

5 tablespoons crème fraîche

165 g plain flour

50 g sugar, plus extra for sprinkling

1 teaspoon baking powder

¼ teaspoon bicarbonate of soda

a pinch of fine sea salt

50 g unsalted butter, cut into small pieces

2–3 tablespoons sugar, for sprinkling

a shallow baking dish, 2–2.5 litres

serves 6

Add a punnet of blackberries to the peaches, if you like, or use a combination of peaches, apricots and blackberries.

peach cobbler

Cut the peaches in half, remove the stones, then cut each half into 3 slices. Put them in the baking dish, sprinkle with the flour and toss well to coat evenly. Add the lemon juice and honey and stir. Set aside.

To make the topping, put the cream and crème fraîche in a large bowl and stir well. Set aside.

Put the flour, sugar, baking powder, bicarbonate of soda and salt in a separate large bowl and mix well. Add the butter and rub it into the flour with your fingertips until the mixture resembles coarse crumbs. Using a fork, stir in the cream mixture until blended – use your hands at the end if necessary, it should be sticky, thick and not willing to blend easily.

Drop spoonfuls of the mixture on top of the peaches, leaving gaps to expose the fruit. Sprinkle sugar liberally on top of the batter. Bake in a preheated oven at 190°C (375°F) Gas 5 until golden, 25–35 minutes. Serve warm with cream or ice cream.

rice pudding

125 g risotto rice, such as arborio

500 ml whole milk, boiled

60 g sugar

1 vanilla pod, split lengthways with a small sharp knife

15 g unsalted butter

a pinch of salt

an ovenproof pan with a lid

serves 4

This is a very simple, classic recipe of which there are many versions. Blanching the rice first removes much of the starch, giving a light, delicate result.

Put the rice in a saucepan with a lid and add cold water to cover. Slowly bring to the boil over medium heat, then boil for 5 minutes. Drain the rice and rinse under cold water. Set aside to drain well.

Meanwhile, put the milk in an ovenproof pan with a lid and bring to the boil. Add the sugar and vanilla pod. Remove from the heat, cover and let stand for 15 minutes. Using the tip of the knife, scrape out the vanilla seeds and stir them through the milk.

Add the rice to the milk, then add the butter and salt. Bring slowly to the boil. Cover and transfer to a preheated oven at 180°C (350°F) Gas 4. Do not stir. Cook until the rice is tender and the liquid is almost completely absorbed but not dry, 25–35 minutes. Serve warm.

apple tart

1 recipe Pâte Brisée
(see page 182)

apple filling

4–5 well-flavoured dessert apples,
peeled and cored

3 tablespoons caster sugar

50 g unsalted butter, cubed

4–6 tablespoons apricot jam

2 tablespoons Calvados
(apple brandy) or brandy

a baking sheet

*a loose-based tart tin,
25 cm diameter*

serves 6-8

Bring the pastry to room temperature. Preheat the oven to 200°C (400°F) Gas 6 and put a baking sheet in the oven to heat.

Roll out the pastry thinly on a lightly floured work surface and use to line the tart tin. Chill or freeze for 15 minutes.

Meanwhile, slice the apples thinly, and coarsely chop up any uneven smaller pieces. Arrange these smaller pieces in the base of the tart. Cover with one-third of the slices any way you like. Arrange the remaining slices neatly in concentric rings over the chopped apples. Sprinkle with the sugar and dot with the butter.

Set the tart tin on the baking sheet and bake in the preheated oven for about 1 hour until the apples are very well browned and the pastry golden. Remove from the oven and transfer to a cooling rack. Wait for 5 minutes, then remove the tart tin.

Put the apricot jam and Calvados in a small saucepan and warm gently. Strain, then use to glaze the apples. Serve at room temperature.

pumpkin pie

This pie is an American classic. Butternut squash purée makes an acceptable substitute if pumpkin is not available. If you can't find canned purée, you can make your own, see note below.

Bring the pastry to room temperature. Preheat the oven to 190°C (375°F) Gas 5.

Roll out the pastry thinly on a lightly floured work surface and use to line the 2 tart tins or pie plates. Trim and crimp or decorate the edges as you wish. Prick the bases all over with a fork, chill or freeze for 15 minutes, then bake blind following the method given on page 182.

Lower the oven to 160°C (325°F) Gas 3.

Put all the filling ingredients in a food processor and blend until smooth. Pour into the pastry cases, set on a baking sheet, and bake for about 1 hour or until just set. Remove from the oven and let stand for 10 minutes, then remove the tart tins and let cool for a few minutes. Serve warm or at room temperature, not chilled.

*Note To make the purée, cut a pumpkin or butternut squash into large chunks. Put in a roasting tin and bake in a preheated oven at 160°C (325°F) Gas 3 for about 1 hour. Scrape the flesh from the skin and purée until smooth in a food processor.

1 recipe American Pie Crust dough
(see page 182)

pumpkin filling

500 ml homemade pumpkin purée* or one 475 g can

100 g light soft brown sugar

3 large eggs

200 ml evaporated milk

120 ml golden syrup

a good pinch of salt

1 teaspoon cinnamon

½ teaspoon mixed spice

1 teaspoon real vanilla essence

2 tablespoons rum (optional)

*2 tart tins or pie plates,
22 cm diameter*

a baking sheet

makes two 22 cm pies

This famous pie comes from the South of the USA – it is supposed to look like the thick, dark, muddy waters of the Mississippi Delta. It is very easy to make and is perfect for sharing with family and friends.

mississippi mud pie

biscuit base

225 g digestive or wheaten biscuits

60 g unsalted butter

60 g plain chocolate, finely chopped

chocolate filling

180 g plain chocolate, chopped

180 g unsalted butter, cut into small pieces

4 large eggs, beaten

90 g light muscovado sugar

90 g dark muscovado sugar

180 ml double cream

chocolate cream

140 ml double cream, well chilled

3 tablespoons cocoa powder

40 g icing sugar

a springform cake tin, 23 cm diameter, well buttered

serves 8

To make the base, put the biscuits in a food processor and blend until fine crumbs form. Alternatively, put the biscuits in a plastic bag and crush with a rolling pin. Transfer the crumbs to a mixing bowl.

Put the butter and chocolate in a heatproof bowl set over a saucepan of steaming but not boiling water and melt gently (do not let the base of the bowl touch the water). Remove from the heat, stir gently, then stir into the biscuit crumbs. When well mixed, transfer the mixture to the prepared tin and, using the back of a spoon, press onto the base and about halfway up the sides of the tin. Chill in the refrigerator while making the filling.

To make the filling, put the chocolate and butter in a heatproof bowl set over a saucepan of steaming but not boiling water and melt gently (do not let the base of the bowl touch the water). Remove from the heat, stir gently, then let cool.

Put the eggs and sugars in a large mixing bowl and, using an electric whisk or mixer, whisk until thick and foamy. Whisk in the cream followed by the melted chocolate. Pour the mixture into the biscuit case and bake in a preheated oven at 180°C (350°F) Gas 4 for about 45 minutes until just firm. Let cool for a few minutes, then remove from the tin.

To make the chocolate cream, put the cream in a mixing bowl, then sift the cocoa and icing sugar on top and stir gently with a wooden spoon until blended. Cover and chill for 2 hours.

Serve the pie at room temperature with the chocolate cream. The pie can be made up to 2 days in advance and kept, well covered, in the refrigerator. Remove from the refrigerator 30 minutes before serving.

BAKING

Home baking is very rewarding. Not only is the smell
so homely and appealing, the results are deliciously
tempting. From cakes and biscuits to bread, there is
nothing quite as enticing as home-baked treats, and
you don't need to spend hours in the kitchen to make
them. Fresher, tastier and better for you than shop-
bought equivalents, there really is no better reason
to put on your new apron and get baking.

175 g self-raising flour

a pinch of salt

a good pinch of
bicarbonate of soda

115 g unsalted butter, very soft

60 g caster sugar

60 g light muscovado sugar

½ teaspoon real vanilla essence

1 large egg, lightly beaten

175 g plain chocolate chunks
or chocolate chips

75 g walnut or pecan pieces

several baking sheets, greased

makes 24

These are always popular and very hard to beat!
Use plain chocolate broken up into chunks or
a bag of chocolate chips.

classic choc chip cookies

Put all the ingredients in a large bowl and mix thoroughly with a wooden spoon. Drop heaped teaspoons of the mixture onto the prepared baking sheets, spacing them well apart.

Bake in a preheated oven at 190°C (375°F) Gas 5 for 8–10 minutes until lightly coloured and just firm.

Remove from the oven and let cool on the baking sheets for 2 minutes or until firm enough to transfer to a wire rack. Let cool completely.

Store in an airtight container and eat within 5 days or freeze for up to 1 month.

These cookies have double the chocolate – there's melted chocolate as well as chunks of plain or white chocolate.

giant double chocolate nut cookies

Put the chopped chocolate in a heatproof bowl set over a saucepan of barely simmering water and melt gently (do not let the base of the bowl touch the water). Remove the bowl from the heat and let cool.

Meanwhile, using a wooden spoon or electric mixer, beat the butter until creamy. Add the sugars and beat again until light and fluffy. Gradually beat in the egg and vanilla essence, followed by the melted chocolate. Sift the flour, salt and baking powder into the bowl and stir. When thoroughly mixed, stir in the nuts and chocolate chunks. Put heaped tablespoons of the mixture, spaced well apart, onto the prepared baking sheets.

Bake in a preheated oven at 180°C (350°F) Gas 4 for 12–15 minutes until just firm. Remove from the oven and let cool on the sheets for 2 minutes or until firm enough to transfer to a wire rack. Let cool completely.

Store in an airtight container and eat within 1 week. The cookies can be frozen for up to 1 month.

140 g plain chocolate, chopped

100 g unsalted butter,
at room temperature

80 g golden caster sugar

80 g dark brown muscovado sugar

1 large egg, beaten

½ teaspoon vanilla essence

150 g plain flour

a pinch of salt

½ teaspoon baking powder

50 g pecan nuts or walnuts, chopped

100 g plain or white chocolate,
chopped into chunks

several baking sheets, greased

makes 16

Brownies are everyone's favourite chocolate indulgence. They're not complicated to make, the most important rule is to aim for the right texture – just set on top, but wonderfully gooey on the inside.

chocolate & cinnamon brownies

75 g hazelnuts

275 g dark chocolate (at least 70 per cent cocoa solids)

225 g unsalted butter

3 eggs

225 g caster sugar

75 g self-raising flour

2 teaspoons ground cinnamon

100 g white chocolate chips

a baking tin, 18 x 28 cm, greased and base-lined

serves 8–12

Put the hazelnuts in a dry frying pan and toast over medium heat until aromatic. Do not let them burn. Let cool, then chop them coarsely.

Put the chocolate and butter in a heatproof bowl set over a saucepan of barely simmering water and melt gently (do not let the base of the bowl touch the water). Remove the bowl from the heat. Put the eggs and sugar in a separate bowl and, using a wooden spoon or electric hand mixer, beat until pale. Stir in the melted chocolate, flour, cinnamon, chocolate chips and chopped nuts.

Spoon the mixture into the prepared tin and bake in a preheated oven at 190°C (375°F) Gas 5 for 35–40 minutes until the top is set but the mixture still feels soft underneath. Remove from the oven and let cool in the tin. Serve cut into squares.

blueberry lemon pound cake

250 g unsalted butter, at room temperature

250 g caster sugar

grated zest of 1 large unwaxed lemon

4 large eggs, at room temperature

a pinch of salt

250 g self-raising flour

75 g dried blueberries

icing sugar, for dusting

a daisy tin, a non-stick cake tin, 27 x 18 cm, or a roasting tin, greased

makes 1 cake

Put the butter in an electric mixer and beat at low speed until creamy. Increase the speed and gradually beat in the sugar, followed by the lemon zest.

Put the eggs and salt in a jug, beat lightly, then add to the creamed mixture, 1 tablespoon or so at a time, beating well after each addition. Add 1 tablespoon flour with the 2 last portions of egg to prevent the mixture from separating.

Sift the rest of the flour onto the mixture and gently fold in with a large metal spoon. When you no longer see streaks of flour, mix in the blueberries.

Transfer the mixture to the prepared tin and spread evenly. Bake in a preheated oven at 180°C (350°F) Gas 4 for about 40 minutes or until a skewer inserted in the centre comes out clean. Remove from the oven, let cool in the tin for 10 minutes, then carefully turn out onto a wire rack to cool completely. Dust with icing sugar before serving.

Store in an airtight container and eat within 5 days.

walnut cake
with coffee syrup

Coffee and walnuts are wonderful together. Drizzling the nutty sponge with a coffee syrup leaves it deliciously moist and gooey.

6 eggs, separated (see page 147)
175 g caster sugar
175 g walnuts, finely ground
75 g fresh, day-old breadcrumbs
whipped cream, to serve

coffee syrup
300 ml strong black coffee
100 g caster sugar
3 star anise

*23 cm springform cake tin,
greased and base-lined*

serves 8

Put the egg yolks in a large bowl, add 125 g of the sugar and whisk until pale. Stir in the ground walnuts and breadcrumbs. (The mixture will be very stiff at this stage.)

Whisk the egg whites in a separate bowl until soft peaks form, then gradually whisk in the remaining sugar. Stir a large spoonful of the whisked egg whites into the cake mixture, then fold in the rest until evenly mixed. Spoon into the prepared cake tin and bake in a preheated oven at 180°C (350°F) Gas 4 for 35–40 minutes until risen and springy to the touch. Remove from the oven and leave the cake in the tin.

Meanwhile, put the coffee, sugar and star anise in a saucepan. Heat until the sugar dissolves, then boil for 5–6 minutes until syrupy. Let cool slightly.

Using a cocktail stick, spike the cake all over the surface, then drizzle with half the syrup. Set aside to cool slightly. Serve the cake still warm with lightly whipped cream and the remaining coffee syrup.

yoghurt cake

The yoghurt pot is the measure, so it doesn't really matter what size – or flavour – you use, but plain, French-style set yoghurt works well.

125 g plain set yoghurt
2 pots sugar
3 pots flour
2 eggs
1 tablespoon sunflower oil
1 teaspoon bicarbonate of soda
a pinch of salt
freshly squeezed juice of 1 orange
1 tablespoon icing sugar, to decorate

a deep cake tin, 23 cm diameter, greased

serves 8

Empty the yoghurt into a large bowl and wipe out the pot so when you measure the other ingredients, they won't stick. Add the sugar, flour, eggs, oil, bicarbonate of soda, salt and half the orange juice. Stir well.

Pour the mixture into the prepared cake tin and bake in a preheated oven at 180°C (350°F) Gas 4 until a knife inserted in the centre comes out clean, 15–20 minutes. Remove from the oven and pierce a few holes in the top with a fork. Pour over the remaining orange juice. Let cool slightly, then turn out onto a wire rack to cool.

Lightly dust with icing sugar and serve the cake at room temperature.

Variation Instead of orange, try other flavourings, such as cinnamon, honey, vanilla, chocolate chunks or fruit pieces.

french almond cake

110 g unsalted butter, softened

150 g caster sugar

3 large eggs, beaten

90 g ground almonds

40 g self-raising flour

1 tablespoon milk or kirsch

1 tablespoon flaked almonds, for sprinkling

icing sugar, for dusting

a sandwich tin, 20 cm diameter, greased and base-lined

makes 1 cake

Serve this traditional French sponge cake with tea or coffee, or for pudding with cherries or berries and cream.

Put the butter, sugar and eggs in a large bowl, add the almonds, flour and milk, then beat with an electric mixer or whisk. When the mixture is quite light and fluffy, spoon it into the prepared tin and spread evenly. Sprinkle the flaked almonds over the top.

Bake in a preheated oven at 180°C (350°F) Gas 4 for 30–35 minutes or until the sponge just springs back when lightly pressed. Run a round-bladed knife around the inside edge of the tin to loosen the sponge, then turn it out onto a wire rack and let cool. Dust with icing sugar before serving. Store in an airtight container and eat within 5 days.

thanksgiving cranberry bundt

filling

60 g whole blanched almonds

150 g fresh cranberries

2 teaspoons ground cinnamon

85 g light muscovado sugar

batter

110 g unsalted butter, at room temperature

2 large eggs, at room temperature, beaten

160 g light muscovado sugar

225 ml sour cream

40 g finely chopped almonds

325 g plain flour

1 teaspoon ground cinnamon

½ teaspoon bicarbonate of soda

1 teaspoon baking powder

icing sugar, for dusting

a Bundt tin, 23 cm diameter, well greased, or a 900 g loaf tin, greased and lined

makes 1 Bundt cake or loaf cake

Make the filling first. Put the almonds in a food processor and chop finely to make a very coarse powder (rather than using shop-bought ground almonds). Transfer to a large bowl. Put the cranberries in the processor and chop coarsely. Add to the almonds, then add the cinnamon and sugar and mix well. Set aside.

To make the batter, put the soft butter, eggs, sugar, sour cream and chopped almonds in another large bowl. Beat with an electric mixer or whisk on medium speed until very smooth. Sift the flour, cinnamon, bicarbonate of soda and baking powder onto the mixture, then stir in with a large metal spoon. When thoroughly mixed, spoon half the batter into the prepared tin. Sprinkle the cranberry mixture over the batter, then top with the rest of the batter.

Bake in a preheated oven at 180°C (350°F) Gas 4 for about 50 minutes or until a skewer inserted into the thickest part of the cake comes out clean. Let cool in the tin for 15 minutes, then carefully turn out onto a wire rack. Dust with icing sugar and let cool completely. Store in an airtight container and eat within 4 days.

Variation Use fresh blueberries instead of cranberries. Make the batter as in the main recipe, but omit the cinnamon and add the grated zest of ½ unwaxed lemon. To make the filling, mix 200 g fresh blueberries with 85 g light muscovado sugar, 60 g chopped almonds and the grated zest of ½ unwaxed lemon. Proceed as in the main recipe.

'Focaccia' literally means 'a bread that was baked on the hearth', but it is easy to bake in conventional ovens. It is found in many different forms, and can be thin and crisp, thick and soft, round or square. This one is made in a tin, but it can be shaped on a baking sheet to any shape you want. A terracotta bakestone ('testa') or unglazed terracotta floor tile heated in the oven will give pizzas and 'focacce' extra lift and a crisp base. Although a rustic focaccia can be made with any basic pizza dough, the secret of a truly light focaccia lies in three risings, and dimpling the dough with your fingers so it traps olive oil while it bakes. Serve with olive oil and balsamic vinegar for dipping and a handful of olives.

focaccia

750 g Italian '00' flour or plain white flour, plus extra for kneading

½ teaspoon fine salt

25 g fresh yeast (for dried yeast, follow the packet instructions)

150 ml good olive oil

450 ml hand-hot water

coarse sea or crystal salt

sprigs of fresh rosemary

2 shallow cake tins, pie or pizza plates, 25 cm diameter, lightly oiled

a water spray

makes 2 thick focacce, 25 cm diameter

Sift the flour and salt into a large bowl and make a hollow in the centre. Crumble in the yeast. Pour in 3 tablespoons of the olive oil, then rub in the yeast until the mixture resembles fine breadcrumbs. Pour in the hand-hot water and mix with your hands until the dough comes together.

Transfer the dough to a floured work surface, wash and dry your hands and knead for 10 minutes until smooth and elastic. The dough should be quite soft, but if too soft to handle, knead in more flour, 1 tablespoon at a time. Put the dough in a clean, oiled bowl, cover with a damp tea towel or clingfilm and let rise in a warm place until doubled in size, 30 minutes–1½ hours.

Knock back the dough and cut it in half. Put on a floured work surface and shape each half into a ball. Roll out into 2 circles, 25 cm diameter, and put in the tins. Cover with a damp tea towel or clingfilm and let rise for 30 minutes.

Remove the tea towel or clingfilm and, using your fingertips, make dimples all over the surface of the dough. They can be quite deep. Pour over the remaining oil and sprinkle generously with salt. Cover again and let rise for 30 minutes. Spray with water, sprinkle the rosemary on top and bake in a preheated oven at 200°C (400°F) Gas 6 for 20–25 minutes. Transfer to a wire rack to cool. Eat the same day or freeze immediately. Serve as bread with a meal, or as a snack with oil, vinegar and olives as suggested in the recipe introduction.

DRINKS

The idea of throwing a glamorous and sophisticated drinks party at home might seem a daunting one, but it needn't be. Make sure you have the necessary equipment, such as glasses, cocktail shakers and barspoons, and enough ingredients to keep the party flowing. Keep things simple by serving just one or two cocktails and always have something exciting for those guests who don't want to drink alcohol.

mojito

Rum is a wonderful base for some great summer cocktails.

5 sprigs of fresh mint
50 ml golden rum
a dash of freshly squeezed lime juice
2 dashes of sugar syrup (see note page 172)
crushed ice
soda water

serves 1

Put the mint in a highball glass, add the rum, lime juice and sugar syrup and pound with a barspoon until the aroma of the mint is released. Add the crushed ice and stir vigorously until the mixture and the mint is spread evenly. Top with soda water and stir again. Serve with straws.

cosmopolitan

This classic cocktail is easy to make and perfect for a crowd.

8 shots of vodka,
25 ml each
750 ml cranberry juice
freshly squeezed juice
of 4 limes
ice cubes

serves 8

Put all the ingredients in a jug and mix. Alternatively, pour the cranberry juice into individual glasses and top with the vodka and lime.

old fashioned

The delicate mix of sugar and orange zest in the classic Old Fashioned will bring to life whichever bourbon you choose to use.

1 white sugar cube
2 dashes of orange bitters
50 ml bourbon
ice cubes
a strip of orange zest

serves 1

Put the sugar cube, soaked with orange bitters, in a rocks glass. Muddle the mixture with a barspoon and add a dash of bourbon and a couple of ice cubes. Keep adding ice and bourbon and keep muddling until the full 50 ml has been added to the glass (ensuring the sugar has dissolved). Rim the glass with some orange zest and drop it into the glass.

sea breeze

Any combination of vodka and freshly squeezed juices will work in creating a Breeze to suit your personal taste.

50 ml vodka
ice cubes
cranberry juice
fresh grapefruit juice
a wedge of lime

serves 1

Pour a large shot of vodka into a highball glass filled with ice. Fill the glass three-quarters full with cranberry juice and top with fresh grapefruit juice. Garnish with a lime wedge and serve with a straw.

classic martini

The classic martini has evolved, in keeping with social tastes, into the ultra-cold, ultra-dry, mostly vodka-based cocktail enjoyed today.

a dash of vermouth (Noilly Prat or Martini Extra Dry)
75 ml chilled gin or vodka
an olive or a lemon twist, to garnish

serves 1

Add the vermouth and gin or vodka to a mixing glass filled with ice and stir. Strain into a frosted martini glass and garnish with an olive or a lemon twist.

french 75

This drink was named after the big artillery gun that the French used during the First World War.

20 ml gin
10 ml freshly squeezed lemon juice
1 barspoon sugar syrup*
chilled champagne, to top up
lemon zest, to garnish

serves 1

Shake the gin, lemon juice and sugar syrup over ice and strain into a champagne flute. Top with champagne and garnish with a long strip of lemon zest.

***Note** To make sugar syrup, stir 500 g sugar into 250 ml water and bring to the boil, stirring vigorously. Let cool and store in the refrigerator.

margarita

All you need to create a decent margarita is good-quality tequila, limes and orange-flavoured liqueur.

50 ml gold tequila
25 ml triple sec (or Cointreau)
freshly squeezed juice of ½ lime
salt, for the glass
cracked ice

serves 1

Shake all the ingredients sharply with cracked ice. Strain into a frosted margarita glass rimmed with salt.

james bond

The James Bond is a variation on the champagne cocktail, using vodka instead of the more traditional brandy.

1 white sugar cube
2 dashes of Angostura bitters
25 ml vodka
champagne, to top up

serves 1

Put the sugar cube in a champagne flute and moisten with Angostura bitters. Add the vodka and top with champagne.

chilled lemongrass tisane

Tisane is the French word for an infusion of herbs, flowers or other aromatics.

1–2 red chillies, deseeded and sliced
2–4 stalks of lemongrass, outer leaves discarded, inner section thinly sliced
5 cm fresh ginger, peeled and sliced
50 g caster sugar
freshly squeezed juice of 2 lemons

to serve
fresh mint leaves
ice cubes

serves 4

Put the chilli in a heatproof jug with the lemongrass, ginger and sugar. Add the lemon juice and 1 litre boiling water and stir to dissolve the sugar. Leave to infuse until cold.

Strain the cooled liquid, then chill it for at least 30 minutes. Serve in tall glasses with mint leaves and ice cubes.

orange & apple refresher

2 large oranges, peeled
2 Granny Smith apples
3 cm fresh ginger, peeled
ice cubes

a juicing machine

serves 2

Push the oranges, apples and ginger through the juicer. Half-fill 2 tall glasses with ice cubes, pour the juice over the top and serve.

virgin mary

Since this variation of the Bloody Mary contains no vodka, you can go a bit crazy on the spices to compensate.

300 ml tomato juice
2 grinds of black pepper
2 dashes of Tabasco sauce
2 dashes of Worcestershire sauce
2 dashes of freshly squeezed lemon juice
1 barspoon horseradish sauce
ice cubes
1 celery stick, to serve

serves 1

Shake all the ingredients (except the celery) over ice and strain into a highball glass filled with ice. Garnish with a stick of celery and serve.

shirley temple

This is a delicious thirst quencher, but only for the very sweet-toothed.

25 ml grenadine
ice cubes
ginger ale or lemonade
a lemon slice, to garnish

serves 1

Pour the grenadine into a glass filled with ice and top with either ginger ale or lemonade. Garnish with a slice of lemon and serve with a straw.

RECIPE BASICS

Here you will find all the essential recipes you will need to refer to again and again, such as Stock, Pastry, Pizza Dough, Sauces and Dressings. Many of them can be bought ready-made, but there is nothing like making your own basic recipes to give your final dish the best flavour and that real home-made touch. Most of these recipes can be made in bulk and frozen or refrigerated for future use.

Too many vegetable stocks are insipid or taste of a single ingredient. This stock may seem extravagant in its use of vegetables, but will have a very good flavour.

vegetable stock

1 large onion, quartered

2 large carrots, quartered

1 small bunch of celery, coarsely chopped (including leaves)

2 leeks, white parts only, halved lengthways, rinsed and halved again

4 courgettes, thickly sliced

2 tomatoes, halved around the middle and seeds squeezed out

1 fennel bulb, quartered

1 cos lettuce heart, coarsely chopped

3 garlic cloves

1 dried red chilli

4 fresh bay leaves

a handful of parsley stalks, crushed

½ lemon, sliced

6 black peppercorns

sea salt, to taste

makes 2-3 litres

Put all the ingredients in a large stockpot. Add water to cover, about 4 litres, and bring to the boil. As soon as it boils, reduce the heat and simmer for 15 minutes. Stir the stock and skim off the foam, then cook at the barest simmer for 1 hour, skimming often.

Remove from the heat and strain the stock into a bowl through a colander lined with muslin. Discard the contents of the colander after they have cooled. Let the stock cool, then refrigerate for several hours.

At this stage you can reboil the stock to concentrate it, or cover and chill in the refrigerator or freeze until needed. The stock will keep in the refrigerator for up to 3 days or can be frozen for up to 6 months.

gravy

This is a thickened gravy for beef which should lightly coat the meat and vegetables.

Put the roasting tin used to cook the meat on top of the stove, heat the reserved 1 tablespoon fat, add the onion and cook slowly over low heat until browned, about 30 minutes. Do not let it burn. Add the cornflour and stock mixture, then season to taste with salt and pepper. Stir constantly over low heat until the mixture boils and simmer for a few minutes. Strain it, or serve it as it is.

1 tablespoon fat from the roasting tin in which the beef or other roast is cooked

1 onion, thinly sliced

250 ml good beef stock, or stock to suit the roast meat or poultry

2 teaspoons cornflour, mixed with 2 teaspoons cold water

sea salt and freshly ground black pepper

serves 4-6

dijon dressing

A simple all-purpose dressing for salads. For a variation, try wholegrain mustard in place of smooth, and experiment with different vinegars.

1 tablespoon Dijon mustard
1 tablespoon white wine vinegar
4 tablespoons extra virgin olive oil
1 garlic clove, crushed
sea salt and freshly ground black pepper

serves 4

Put the mustard, vinegar, oil and garlic in a bowl and mix with a fork or small metal whisk. Add enough water for the consistency you want, 1–2 tablespoons, and salt and black pepper to taste.

horseradish sauce

Grating the horseradish will make your eyes water, but the result is worth it.

1 large horseradish root
1 tablespoon white wine vinegar
250 ml double cream
sea salt

makes 500-600 ml, serves 6-8

Scrape the fresh horseradish root clean and grate it finely to give 2 tablespoons.

Put in a bowl, add the vinegar and salt and stir well. Add the cream and whisk until it becomes thick and light. Let it rest at room temperature for at least 2 hours, but serve the same day.

red onion marmalade

Delicious in burgers, with sausages and cold meat, or on bruschetta with goats' cheese.

2 tablespoons olive oil
750 g red onions, very thinly sliced
1 fresh bay leaf
1 teaspoon fresh thyme leaves
50 g demerara sugar
3 tablespoons balsamic vinegar
150 ml red wine
grated zest and juice of 1 unwaxed orange
sea salt and freshly ground black pepper

serves 8

Heat the oil in a large saucepan until hot. Add the onions, bay leaf and thyme and salt and pepper to taste. Cover with a lid and cook over low heat, stirring occasionally, for 30 minutes until the onions are softened and translucent.

Add the sugar, vinegar, red wine and the orange zest and juice. Cook uncovered for 1½ hours until no liquid is left and the onions are a dark, rich red. Stir frequently during the last 30 minutes to prevent the onions from burning.

Let the mixture cool, then transfer to sterilized jars (see page 4). It will keep refrigerated for several weeks.

chilli oil

300 ml extra virgin olive oil
4 dried red chillies, coarsely chopped

makes 300 ml

Put the oil and chillies in a screw-top jar and let infuse for 2 days before using.

pâte brisée

Sift the flour and salt together onto a sheet of greaseproof paper.

Put the butter and egg yolk in a food processor and blend until smooth. Add the water and blend again. Add the flour and salt and pulse until just mixed.

Transfer to a lightly floured work surface and knead gently until smooth. Form into a ball, flatten slightly and wrap in clingfilm. Chill in the refrigerator for at least 30 minutes.

Let the dough return to room temperature before rolling out.

Baking blind Line the tart case with foil, baking parchment or all-purpose clingfilm (flicking the edges inwards towards the centre so that they don't catch on the pastry), then fill with baking beans. Set on a baking sheet and bake blind in the centre of a preheated oven at 200°C (400°F) Gas 6 for 10–12 minutes. Remove the foil, baking parchment or clingfilm and the baking beans and return the pastry case to the oven for a further 5–7 minutes to dry out completely.

250 g plain flour
1 teaspoon salt
125 g unsalted butter, softened
1 large egg yolk
2½–3 tablespoons iced water

makes about 350 g pastry

american pie crust

This is a recipe for the classic American pie crust. It is a very light, crumbly pastry – similar to shortcrust and very homely. The quantity is enough for two pies. You could make and bake both pies now, freeze all the dough to use later, or make double quantity and freeze it all.

Sift the flour and salt into a large bowl. Cut in the fat using 2 round-bladed knives or a pastry blender (or do this in a food processor).

Put the egg in a separate bowl. Stir in the vinegar or lemon juice, then add the water.

Pour the wet mixture into the dry mixture, then cut it in with the knives or pastry blender.

Bring the dough together quickly using your hands. Knead until smooth, either in the bowl or on a floured work surface. Divide in 2 so it is easier to roll out later. Shape the dough into flattened balls, wrap in clingfilm, then chill for at least 30 minutes before rolling out.

375 g plain flour
a good pinch of salt
250 g white cooking fat, chilled
1 medium egg, beaten
1 tablespoon wine vinegar
or lemon juice
4 tablespoons iced water

makes about 675 g pastry,
enough for 2 deep tart cases,
24 cm diameter

These Yorkshire puddings can be made individually,
or make one big one and cut it into pieces to serve.

yorkshire pudding

275 ml milk

2 eggs

125 g plain flour

½ teaspoon salt

4–6 tablespoons fat from the roasting tin

*1 small roasting tin, 45 x 30 mm,
a 6-hole Yorkshire pudding tray,
or a 12-hole bun tin*

serves 6

Put the milk, eggs, flour and salt in a bowl and whisk well.

Heat the fat on top of the stove in one large tin or divide between 6 holes (1 tablespoon fat each) or 12 holes (½ teaspoon fat). Pour in the batter (take care because it will spatter).

Cook in a preheated oven at 230°C (450°F) Gas 8 until well risen (35 minutes for the large tin or 15 minutes for the individual tins). Serve as soon as possible.

For a really good pizza dough, try to use the superfine durum
wheat '00' flour, which you can buy in Italian stores and large
supermarkets. Otherwise, choose a strong white bread flour.

pizza dough

To make the dough, sift the flour into the bowl of a food mixer fitted with a dough hook attachment or a food processor fitted with a plastic blade. Add the yeast and salt, then work in the oil and water to form a soft dough.

Remove from the bowl and transfer to a floured work surface. Knead for 5 minutes until the dough is smooth. Roll it into a ball and put in an oiled bowl. Cover with clingfilm and let rise for about 45 minutes or until doubled in size. Use as directed in the pizza recipe on page 72.

250 g strong white flour

1 teaspoon easy-blend dried yeast (half a 7 g sachet)

1 teaspoon salt

1 tablespoon extra virgin olive oil, plus extra to serve

125–150 ml hand-hot water

*makes 2 thin-crust pizzas,
20-25 cm diameter*

stockists & sources

index

recipe credits

LAURA WASHBURN trained at the prestigious Paris cooking school, *Ecole de Cuisine La Varenne*, and worked with Patricia Wells, author of *A Food Lover's Guide to Paris*.

Bacon, avocado and feta salad
Beef provençal
Braised pork chops with tomato, orange and chilli
Bulghur wheat pilaff
Butternut squash with pistou
Carrots with cream and herbs
Chicken, asparagus and gorgonzola salad with hazelnuts
Chilli with all the trimmings
Duck breasts with peppercorns
French beans with garlic
French fries
French onion soup
Greek omelette
Lemon-spiced chicken
Linguine, peas, pancetta and sage
Macaroni gratin
Meatballs in red pepper sauce
Moroccan prawns with couscous
Mussels with fennel, tomatoes, garlic and saffron
Sole meunière
Peach Cobbler
Pork chops with piquant sauce
Potato wedges
Rice pudding
Ricotta cake
Rustic pâté with green peppercorns
Savoy cabbage with bacon and cream
Spring lamb stew with vegetables
Tomato salad with anchovy vinaigrette
Whole roast monkfish
Yoghurt cake

LOUISE PICKFORD is a British food writer, now living and working in Sydney. She writes for several magazines and has written a number of cookbooks.

Baked eggs with smoked salmon
Charred asparagus and herb frittata
Chicken panini with mozzarella
Chilled lemongrass tisane
Chilli oil
Chilli spiked cornbread
Chocolate and cinnamon brownies
Cinnamon-soaked granola
Creamy eggs with rocket pesto
Eggs benedict
Fresh figs with ricotta and honeycomb
Hash browns with sausages
Mushrooms on toast with cheese
Orange and apple refresher
Pan-fried fillet steak with horseradish butter
Parma-wrapped pork
Peppered tuna with salsa rossa
Prawn fried rice
Prawns with chilli oil
Tex-mex pork rack
Tomato pizza with capers and anchovies
Waffles with maple syrup ice cream
Walnut cake with coffee syrup

LESLEY WATERS is one of the best-known television chefs and teacher-cooks in Britain. She is a star of TV cooking on the BBC's *Ready Steady Cook*.

Bloody Mary
Classic creamy mashed potato
Coq au vin
Dijon dressing
Green Thai vegetable curry
Lamb steaks with coriander cumin crust
Mediterranean fish stew
Orange and bitter chocolate muffins
Pan-grilled bruschetta with onion marmalade and goats' cheese
Peppered goats' cheese
Peppered sage pork with pasta
Pizza topping suggestions
Red onion marmalade
Roasted potatoes
Seared peppered beef salad
Seared scallops with brittle parma
Seared swordfish with avocado and salsa
Tropical smoothie
Very berry smoothie
Warm chunky fish pâté
Wholegrain mustard tarragon chicken
Whole roasted chicken

MAXINE CLARK teaches at Alastair Little's Tasting Places in Sicily and Tuscany. Her work appears regularly in magazines.

American pie crust dough
Apple tart
Barbecued salmon fillets
Foccacia
Gorgonzola and ricotta risotto
Italian mixed salad
Lasagne
Pâte brisée
Pizza dough
Pumpkin pie
Salmon, dill and Parmesan tart
Tiramisu
Traditional New York cheesecake
Vegetable stock

FRAN WARDE trained as a chef and ran a successful restaurant, and catering business. She is now a freelance food writer.

Beef en croute with mustard sauce
Cosmopolitan
Making coffee
Making the perfect cup of tea
Mashed minty potatoes and peas
Onion tart with tomato salsa
Raspberries in champagne jelly
Risotto primavera
Salade niçoise
Smoked haddock chowder
Smoked wild salmon and scrambled eggs with avruga
Spicy-crust roasted rack of lamb
Steak and tomato sandwich

BEN REED was named Cocktail Bartender of the Year in 1997 in a competition sponsored by Absolut Vodka.

Classic Martini
French 75
James Bond
Margarita
Mojito
Old fashioned
Sea breeze
Shirley Temple
Virgin Mary

LINDA COLLISTER'S books on baking have sold over 500,000 copies worldwide.

Blueberry lemon pound cake
Chocolate chip cookies
French almond cake
Giant double choc nut cookies
Mississippi mud pie
Thanksgiving cranberry bundt

SONIA STEVENSON is one of Britain's great chefs. She often appears on TV, and is a judge on BBC's *Masterchef*.

Gravy
Horseradish sauce
Roast beef
Traditional fish pie
Tuna with paprika crumbs
Yorkshire puddings

CLARE FERGUSON has been the Food Editor of *Elle* and *She* magazines and is the author of many books.

Apricot and orange gelato
Aubergine antipasto with pine nuts
Bitter chocolate and hazelnut gelato
Penne with mozzarella
Spanish potato omelette

CELIA BROOKS BROWN is one of the talented teacher-chefs at the bookshop, Books For Cooks, in Notting Hill, London.

Blueberry muffins
Pancakes
Raspberry roulade
Tuscan panzanella

LINDY WILDSMITH is well known from her appearances in the celebrity kitchen at *House & Garden* fairs. She also has her own cooking school.

Quick Neapolitan tomato sauce
Ragù
Spaghetti alla carbonara
Spaghetti with baby clams

JANE NORAIKA is head chef at London's most celebrated vegetarian restaurant, *Food for Thought*.

Leek, feta and black olive tart
Roasted vegetable dauphinois

LINDA TUBBY is a leading London food writer and food stylist. Her work appears in a number of magazines.

Hake in green sauce
Oysters rockefeller

MANISHA GAMBHIR HARKINS is Features Editor of *The Master's Table* magazine and was the Guild of Food Writers' Food Journalist of the Year in 1999.

Butternut squash soup with allspice and pine nuts

photography credits

Key: a=above, b=below, r=right, l=left, c=centre.

Martin Brigdale
Pages 39, 41, 43, 44, 48, 52, 69c, 82, 89, 94, 96, 97, 98, 111, 112, 116, 117, 119, 122, 123, 128, 142, 143, 145, 151, 153, 154, 167, 177c, 178, 179, 182, 183, 184, 188

Peter Cassidy
Pages 1, 4–5, 7br, 9c, 16, 24, 28, 36, 40, 46, 58, 60, 61, 62, 65, 73, 77, 87, 91c, 93, 102, 106, 113, 115, 132, 138, 157c, 160, 168, 169l, 174, 177l, 180

Debi Treloar
Pages 13l, 14c, 14-15, 18, 19, 32, 37, 50, 55, 59, 68, 101, 105, 125r, 127, 141l, 144, 169c, 171

Polly Wreford
Endpapers, pages 3c, 3r, 7ar, 7bl, 9l, 12al, 17l, 69l, 90, 91l, 107l, 107r, 124, 186, 190, 191, 192

David Munns
Pages 13r, 47, 51c, 54, 57, 66, 81, 85, 86, 99, 107c, 120, 134, 135, 136, 139, 149, 150

Ian Wallace
Pages 20, 23, 26, 27, 29, 30, 31, 78, 156, 157r, 163

William Lingwood
Pages 13c, 74, 108, 109, 169r, 170, 172, 173, 175

David Brittain
Pages 2, 3l, 8, 14l, 34, 35r, 69r, 177r

Nicky Dowey
Pages 53, 70, 71, 131

David Loftus
Pages 17r, 51r, 140, 187

Diana Miller
Pages 157l, 159, 161, 164

Alan Williams
Pages 6, 7al, 11c, 125l

Dan Duchars
Pages 17c, 141c, 141r

Chris Everard
Pages 9r, 10, 12r

Noel Murphy
Pages 12bl, 35l, 189

Andrew Wood
Pages 11a, 15, 176

Jan Baldwin
Pages 35c, 91r

Philip Webb
Pages 45, 146

Caroline Arber
Page 51l

Christopher Drake
Page 11b

Francesca Yorke
Page 125c

picture credits

Page 10 the London apartment of the Sheppard Day Design Partnership (020 7821 2002)

Page 12r an apartment in Milan designed by Nicoletta Marazza, interior designer (+39 02760 14482 by appointment)

Page 50 Kristiina Ratia and Jeff Gocke's family home in Norwalk, Connecticut (Kristiina Ratia Designs (+1 203-852-0027)